MISSING PIECES

MISSING PIECES

A Collection of Essays

Christopher Kunz

*This book is dedicated to my wife, Ellen,
my family—Julie, Al, Michelle, Therese, and Mark—
and my community of friends*

Contents

Edge Pieces

-define the border and give the puzzle shape-

The hardest task in life is to change ourselves;

it's only natural to first wait for the world to change

in the hope that we won't have to.

"Monsters Under the Bed"

Mom's Lessons

My mom never stops trying to teach me new lessons. She didn't stop when I thought I knew it all in college. She certainly isn't going to stop now just because she's no longer alive. We had an agreement: she could give me all the advice she wanted as long as I didn't have to follow it. That arrangement worked great when she was alive, but now she has more resources and a bigger stage.

I drive by the hospital almost every day. Most times I hardly notice the stately building, but occasionally I see my mom on the roof waving her arms to get my attention. The lighting is usually just right to see inside the rooms and I think about the difficult decisions being made there. I realize, hidden in plain sight, patients are tethered to machines, waiting for test results that might not bring good news, while I drive past lamenting my water bill.

Other times I am just minding my own business in an uneventful day reading a book or making dinner. I am neither happy nor sad and could be doing any of a million other things. In these quiet moments, when life can slip by so quickly, I hear my mom whisper in my ear, "Hey kid, enjoy this moment. This is life."

If I feel uneasy because I can't control a situation, I hear her laugh. The harder I try to make someone do what I want, the more I see her face, with that knowing smile, gently reminding me that we are here as the entertainment; we don't run the show. I have a part to play, so I bow to my mom in the audience and play with gusto.

She also shows me how to work the system. When I go clothes shopping with my wife, I'm ready to leave before my wife has even tried on her first item. My mom is playing in the clothes racks with the kids and pokes her head out, handing me a shirt my wife would love. I give her a look to indicate she's not helping, but she explains the more I help, the faster I can leave. Soon I have a handful of cute tops as I scrounge shelves for my wife's size. In the flurry of activity, I discover purpose and a little inner peace, which aren't bad items to find while shopping.

I catch myself judging people. Whether I only think it or say it out loud, I critique body shapes, personal preferences, and tattoo placement. I am annoyed by the overuse of drive-thrus and make rules about grocery cart use. My mom laughs, not with me, but at me. Apparently, nothing is funnier where she comes from. It's like watching a dog chase its tail. The more we find faults in others, the faster we spin in circles.

In troubling times with natural disasters, political unrest, and financial chaos, it's easy to get discouraged thinking of what-ifs. My mom shows up like a relief worker dishing out wisdom. These moments have all been lived before, now is simply your turn to experience them. Disaster has struck in every way imaginable. The only difference is how close we are to the epicenter. Politics, like financial climates, moves in waves, crashing to shore only to recede with time.

My mom's absence is a stronger force than her unexpected appearances. It's a constant reminder that our time is limited. I didn't believe parents could die, just as I believe I'll never die. This isn't the invincibility of a teenager, but more the bewilderment of someone who has crested the middle of his journey and still can't recognize what's on the other side.

There are so many lessons my mom hasn't yet taught me. I can imagine the clues flying through the air, literally bouncing off my forehead. She's sitting back watching with the patience of a mother of three older children, knowing I will learn when I'm ready. Meanwhile the universe peppers me with answers.

Last night's sunset was no doubt loaded with messages and my mom's mantra comes to me, "Throw it out to the universe." Whether the problem was polluted groundwater, how to pay for a new roof, or running out of eggs, her advice was always the same. The theory goes that everything you need is in the universe if: you release your problems into it, the universe will provide the solution, as long as you are ready to accept it.

Now I can't look at a sunset or tree without wondering what they are trying to say, like trying to understand a six-month-old expressing her ideas. For all I know maybe the six-month-old is screaming the answer, "Hey, I just came from there. Relax and enjoy the ride. It all works out in the end." But I never learned to speak Universe.

I want to know what the future holds, but at the same time I cover my eyes from the gory details. Perhaps the universe doesn't think I'm ready, even if my mom put in a good word. I certainly have my doubts. I've asked for hints, but apparently the answers are right in front of me. I'm looking in the wrong direction.

I'll keep searching for clues and looking for the right angle to see around my fears. Meanwhile my mom will continue giving me advice, and I will pretend I'm not listening. But we both know better.

- 2013 -

Young Gamblers

Growing up, my family didn't play Parcheesi or checkers. We played poker. We gathered 'round Friday nights with our loose change in hand, swapping pennies for poker chips and bored looks for game faces. We played for hours, learning different poker games and strategies, but the biggest lesson was what poker taught us: everything isn't as it seems.

Just exchanging coins for chips was an experience. I learned to fish coins from my piggy bank that was designed only to be broken open. Ah, the life of a gambler. Dad had an affinity for change and a seemingly endless supply. Every single school day, my dad had four piles of lunch money resting on the fireplace in different but exact amounts for each one of us kids. Mom had her own unique style, fishing coins from the bottom of her duffle-bag-like purse. It was easy to tell which nickels and dimes were hers. They were caked with a combination of tobacco, makeup, and purse lint.

With chips in hand, the fun began. Poker forced us to look each other in the eye, if only to get a hint of the cards we each held. Our family never paid closer attention than when pennies were on the line. Victory depended on being able to discern if that smirk on my sister's face was high school hijinks or a hidden pair of aces.

Everyone bluffed from time to time. It was a chance to lie and get away with it. Mom always knew when we didn't have the cards, but folded anyway. She had watched our faces so many times when we told her we didn't break the lamp or we were at a friend's house that she could identify and categorize every line and gesture of dishonesty.

Mom seldom bluffed, but if she did, nobody called her on it. It was inconceivable she would deceive us. We were young and naïve. We didn't understand parents have just as many secrets and usually more. They just have better poker faces.

Dad liked to introduce new poker games, the more outlandish the better, which is how we came to play Night Baseball Rained Out. It's a seven-card game with threes and nines wild and fours get you an extra card—that's baseball. It's a night game meaning you can't look at your cards which are all dealt face down. Finally, the game is rained out and must start over if the king of spades shows up. It took forever to play, relied mostly on luck, and produced monster pots.

Dad always commented while dealing with a "Two, no help" and a "Club, possible flush"—maybe to help us understand the game. But more likely Dad enjoyed, as most fathers do, describing the world around him like a sports commentator, with millions hanging on his every word. His running comments became the backdrop for numerous other conversations, some to gain insight into a player's hand while others were to gain knowledge into us.

By channeling all of our energy into maintaining the perfect poker face, we were often susceptible to questions that fell below our gambling radar. When raking in my winnings, I might have hidden the fact that I had three buried clubs, but I failed to conceal how my day went at school.

We were just happy to be gambling like adults. Being the youngest, I was always torn between the purchasing power of the penny and not wanting to be left out of a single hand. My older siblings felt like high rollers on the Vegas strip as they learned lingo like *full boat*, *trips*, and *ladies*, raising Dad's bet with a nonchalant flick of the wrist and steely-eyed gaze of a professional gambler. I tried to mimic that gaze and would have succeeded if I hadn't been busy crying because I lost the last hand.

Conversations were different on poker night, as was the atmosphere. It was like spying on our parents. We heard about how their day went instead of the other way around. My dad told jokes he heard at the office. They usually had complicated storylines building up to a convoluted punch line like, "Pardon me Roy, is that the cat that ate your new shoes?" delivered to the "Chattanooga Choo Choo" melody.

The deal went around the table as we each took turns calling the shots. We'd name the game, deal the cards, and slowly transition power from parents to kids. We weren't just following rules; we were defining them as we became gamblers. We learned to read faces, make decisions based on limited information, and understand the odds.

I still play cards on Friday nights with similar antique poker chips. I play with my in-laws. The cards haven't changed, still fifty-two, but I am different. I seldom cry when I don't win, and I miss the complicated jokes and tobacco infused nickels.

I hear new stories now and the card game often changes from poker to Sheepshead or Naples, but the intimacy of playing cards at the kitchen table remains. The cards are comfortable and the company always welcome. Ante up.

- 2014 -

The Power of Neighbors

Neighbors are strange people. I should know: I am one. We see them at their worst—in their PJs with bed head retrieving the morning newspaper, using their outdoor voice with their kids, or gardening in their ripped jeans and favorite twenty-year-old t-shirt. The rest of the world may know them as sharp-dressed professionals, but we know otherwise. We also see them at their best—lending a helping hand, taking care of kids, or welcoming friends and family.

Just like family, we don't choose our neighbors. So if we have a neighbor who likes riding a unicycle, we try to be encouraging while hoping no one else finds out. If they have the wrong political sign in their yard, we refrain from swiping it in the middle of the night. In exchange for some quirky attributes we get entertainment, new friendships, and fodder for an article. Besides, my neighbors probably secretly complain about my brightly painted garage that no longer matches the house.

Neighbors can be handy too. There's always that one person in the neighborhood who has every tool and gadget. If you need a welding torch, no problem. Chop saw with special heavy-duty metal cutting blade: he has two. Pneumatic nailing gun—what size cartridge do you need? You find yourself taking on new and impossible projects just to see if a tool exists that your neighbor doesn't have. I wonder if he has a backhoe to dig a pond?

House projects completely change the dynamics of the neighborhood. Like feeling compelled to touch a pregnant woman's belly, we feel the need to examine, critique, and investigate all neighborhood projects. If you truly want to meet your neighbors, redo your kitchen or put on an addition. Your house becomes public property making your yard the new playground and community center for the neighborhood.

As much as we know about our neighbors, there is plenty we don't. I think one of my neighbors is a secret CIA agent. She tried to tell me the huge truck in the driveway was for the guy building a bookcase. It's more likely he was building a concealed spy headquarters. I don't believe for a minute that their van doesn't have all the eavesdropping upgrades. And the weekly "UPS" deliveries? Please. With all of her spy tools, she can probably see me typing this article right now. Or maybe she's already done a psychological profile on me and knew I'd write this article even before I did. I make sure I'm always nice to her, just in case.

Of course, the beauty of neighbors is that we don't know everything about them and we never will. So, it's fun to discover something new. Who would have thought our quiet mild-mannered neighbor with the two kids always wanted to be a roller derby queen? It makes me wonder what other stories are lurking in the neighborhood.

Like bears, neighbors hibernate in the winter. I'll go months without seeing a single neighbor. How they sneak out of the house without me seeing them, I'll never know. Eventually, as the snowbanks melt and the first lawn mower fires up, all my neighbors migrate outside like a herd of elk. We comment on the height of the kids and catch up on news as if we lived in another country instead of a few feet away.

Neighbors remind us that we aren't alone. If we are feeling under the weather or isolated, the sound of kids running around next door or the sight of a family walking past can help center us on this spinning planet of six billion people. Being a neighbor is not about the big gestures but the simple connections—a light left on, a wave, the impromptu conversation on the sidewalk.

Communication and community have changed with blogs and emails. We can easily converse with people around the world and still forget to connect with the people across the street. As we often tell kids to go outside and play, maybe we should take that same advice. Turn off your TV. Go for a walk. Smile. Say hi.

From relationships based more on proximity than choice, we find a special bond. We learn to appreciate differences and find unique connections. We become neighbors. Besides, who knows when you will need to borrow a backhoe or a good shoe phone.

- 2008 -

Ruthless with Rudbeckia

I need to be more ruthless with the rudbeckia. In early spring I'm not picky, I just want to see something green after all the snow. It's only in fall, after their bright yellow faces have distracted me all summer, that I realize the rudbeckia have invaded the creeping phlox and occupy most of the garden and part of the driveway. When telling gardening stories, rudbeckia is my antagonist.

A gardener must be brutal at times, taking broad strokes and quick action. Plants, like dogs, can sense weakness. When I first bought rudbeckia, I was afraid the soil wasn't right or I'd plant them too deep or rabbits would eat them. They sensed my vulnerability and in turn developed their own secret agenda. Only when the rudbeckia were all but forgotten did they show their faces, coming up everywhere except where I planted them.

They quickly took over, and when I was too tentative to thin them back, they tormented me by attacking my car on a daily basis. I feel guilty when I see their mangled bodies on the driveway, but equally amazed when they spring back in the afternoon for another assault.

It's the misguided goal of gardeners to try to organize nature. We should give plants a poke and get out of the way. I often wonder if nature instead organizes us with a nudge in one direction and a pull in another. Is there a bigger hand tending us or are we like an open prairie, free to run amok?

As a gardener I take a simple approach and allow the hardy plants to take over. I tried regulating my gardens by introducing new plants and discouraging undesirable ones, but I had difficulty judging weeds from plants.

I'm not big on annuals. They are too brash with their high-maintenance and constant need for attention. Perennials don't have quite the pizzazz, but they don't have the attitude either. They wait patiently all winter only to emerge bigger than before, offering up tender shoots from the once-frozen ground. They may wander a bit, lining the sidewalk like spectators preparing for an outdoor concert, but who can blame them for their curiosity?

In early spring each plant looks so lonely. I want to introduce them to other interesting vegetation, but they will make their own friends. Before long the garden will be overcrowded with wild parties and rudbeckia trying to crash every get-together.

It could be worse. I could have gardens filled with quackgrass. Instead I have an invasion of glorious yellow flowers. What am I complaining about? I like variety. I like sedum that bloom before rudbeckia even wakes up or the creeping phlox that create a warm blanket of flowers on cool spring days. I like thyme with its Froot Loop-like smell and Lady's Mantle for its velvety leaves.

I want all these plants and more to find sanctuary in my gardens and not feel bullied by the rudbeckia. If only they could all play nice and respect each other's space while living in harmony as one big mixed-up bouquet.

Life isn't fair and not all plants are equal. Some perform best in shade while others need full sun. It's not that some plants aren't trying, but no matter how hard rosemary works, it can't overwinter in Wisconsin. Daylilies won't bloom in full shade. Every person, like every plant, needs to find the best environment to grow. Failure isn't always about effort as much as it is about conditions.

Maybe my expectations are skewed. I want my gardens to behave by my set of rules. I unilaterally decide weed from plant. I water them. I care for them. If not for me, they wouldn't even exist, yet I can't get one flower to stop invading my driveway.

I can tinker with the soil and move plants around, but I can never create the perfect conditions for all plants to thrive. Conditions change. A tree topples, bringing light where there once was only shade, and with it, opportunity for stunted plants to reach for the sky. Sometimes rudbeckia shields the sun for the jack-in-the-pulpit to flourish and other times it chokes out the sedum.

Perhaps my garden is just as it should be, some plants struggling to survive while others prosper. Or maybe that's just what the rudbeckia wants me to believe.

- 2011 -

Three Friends in a Canoe

I sat in a canoe drifting, talking with two close friends I rarely see. On one level it was a typical day: three people drifting on the water, talking about nothing of great consequence. On another level it was so much more.

It was an opportunity to connect—to gain strength from the power of friendship. Underneath the words was a history: that time I chickened out of kissing a girl in sixth grade and when we won the milk carton boat race. We jumped from topic to topic with ideas springing from all the conversations we never had. Many sentiments still went unsaid, lost in the fumes of longtime friendships. All this, hidden in a quiet conversation that was carried away on the breeze.

It doesn't happen all the time. Not every conversation—even with the best of friends—transports us. These moments are sneaky. Only when we're not looking, with no expectations, do we stumble upon these memorable moments. They hit us so profoundly they become tangible. We collect them like old concert ticket stubs.

It's the imprint of days like these that carry us through the forgettable moments. We gather these strands of bliss and weave them through our lives, strengthening our spirits to withstand those times when we are adrift and life works so hard to prove us wrong.

That day in the canoe, like so many other moments equally benign yet completely life-affirming, not only strengthened my soul, but intertwined my friends' lives with my own existence. I'm not the same person. I've been altered, like adding hot fudge to ice cream.

Distance puts my longtime friends out of reach and I have a hard time wringing hot fudge from the phone. So I try to find additional toppings. I live near some great people, but none that I went on a twenty-hour bus ride to Montana while singing every song we knew. I most likely will never again be an opposing graham cracker to a four-person s'more on Halloween.

Friendships become more difficult as I get older. It's harder for those incredible moments to sneak up on me. I'm always looking over my shoulder—too polite, overly protective. No one makes me pair up in class, I seldom have to share, and I certainly don't want to impose myself.

Our adult lives are so well-measured that I seldom find myself in compromising circumstances. I show neither my weaknesses nor, with a greater accumulation of resources, my vulnerabilities—two major ingredients in creating friendships so deep I still raise my hands in victory when I think about the canoe race we had in the Boundary Waters years ago.

Great friendships usually need a catalyst—some bonding experience that breaks through our protective shells and grabs hold of us—like sledding down an ice-covered hill at Lutsen Ski Resort late at night with two guys on a broiler pan. No barriers can withstand the race to the bottom of the hill.

Roommates are catalysts personified. As we try to parse our lives, separating our public self from the private one, playing to different audiences, the people we live with see the backstage along with costume changes. No matter how great our performance, they know us without makeup or props. They see us when we are no longer acting and in turn, become lifelong fans.

If you have young children, you're lucky. You have your own personal friend finder. Children become the scouts of relationships, forging ahead, making first contact, and acting as liaison. They don't overanalyze a situation or debate the social correctness of an introduction. They barge ahead, asking questions and making demands.

Kids know what they're looking for—someone to play with. We are looking for someone who fits into our complicated set of rules. They are fearless, seeking out connections like a switchboard operator. Each person could be their new best friend. They haven't learned to be the discriminating connoisseur of relationships as adults have. They don't judge the final dish, just the first bite. While we search for perfection, they have sampled the complete smorgasbord.

Friends are essential to life. Studies show they actually help us live longer. They certainly make us happier. Friends help us find those pockets of subtle bliss in our densely packed lives. They let us take them for granted and act like an idiot. They balance these transgressions against a library of our finer moments and deem us worthy of their friendship.

Longtime friends will sit in a canoe and share their lives, helping us bridge the gap between who we were and who we are. New friends allow us to grow, making new connections in an ever-changing world. It's like a hot fudge sundae with whipped cream and nuts. I'm not saying who the nuts are.

- 2010 -

Monsters Under the Bed

Change is scary. It's the big monster that lives under our beds. We lie awake at night afraid of the grip of its hairy arm. We wish it could be explained away with a cute story and reassuring words, but we've seen too much evidence to the contrary—wrinkles, newspaper headlines, new initiatives at the office. The monster is here. The question is, what do we do about it?

I would like to accept change, but it always sneaks up on me. It moves so slowly that twenty years have passed by the time I notice. Though I am forty-six, I don't completely understand that I am forty-six. I see a group of twenty-five-year-olds and think they're just a few years younger than me. I swear most of the Packers football players are older than I am, not young enough to be my sons.

My wife will ask me to describe a person, and I will invariably say something like he was an older gentleman, about my height. She will ask his age, and I'll say mid-to-late-forties. Then she waits for the realization to settle in.

I am not obsessed with age, but I finally realize where this journey is headed and I am not sure if I'll approve of the final accommodations. I'm assured that an impressive list of people has stayed there and the amenities are excellent, but chances are I might end up with a basement suite. Unfortunately, no one can give me a personal recommendation.

I need to learn to dance with change. Change might always lead, but as a good dance partner, I'm expected to respond to subtle cues—a slight pressure on the small of the back, the shift from right to left, the competition's tap on the shoulder. I try to follow, but I often step on toes moving to a different beat.

Routine brings with it comfort and security, but once that's achieved I long for something new. I search for a balance with the familiar and foreign, battling between the need to explore and the desire to put on something comfortable and stay home.

As I get older, familiarity becomes a cozy blanket I like to curl up with. It gets harder to throw off the covers. But like watching a movie on a glorious Saturday afternoon, soon the pendulum swings and I need to accomplish something grand. Is there still time to rake the leaves, wash the car, and write an inspiring article?

Politicians love change as if they invented it. They promise to share their discovery and change the country while leaving us untouched—feeding our belief that everyone else needs to change except us.

If we're not trying to avoid change, then we are mesmerized by it. When we don't like where we are, change is the only boat off the island. We long to turn sixteen, anticipating the freedom of a driver's license. We look forward to our first real job and living on our own so we can feel self-sufficient and finally have everything fall into place. As soon as we get that promotion, we'll spend more time with the kids. Once we retire, we'll take those vacations or start that hobby.

Instead of embracing change we cling to the idea of change. The hardest task in life is to change ourselves; it's only natural to first wait for the world to change in hope that we won't have to. If we can't find some happiness to-day, chances are we're looking in the wrong direction.

Many people believe in the old adage, "If it ain't broke, don't fix it," suggesting some things shouldn't change. But nothing stays the same—not the problems and certainly not the solutions. If I stand still for too long, I just get a longer view of all the things I can't reach.

If my timing is good, I can gracefully change my surroundings, giving the illusion that everything is the same. Like driving next to a train going the same speed, nothing seems to move, yet I'm still hurtling towards my destination. When I change in synch with my wife, we look the same as the day we got married and our future looks long and bright, especially if my wife is wearing her reading glasses.

Change might be a monster, but it's my monster. When not neglected or abused, it can actually lead the way, forcing me to shed my security blanket and look under the bed. As always, I am too slow to see anything, but while I am up, I might as well reorganize my eight-track collection.

- 2010 -

Cleaning Out the Closet

For the third morning in a row, the temperature remained stubbornly below zero. The wind blew, the house moaned, and in this torture chamber of an environment, I was feeling ruthless. Only one thing can be done when feeling this way—clean out the closet. So it started on a Saturday morning as I stared at my clothes spilling from their shelves. I thought this would only take a couple of minutes.

First, I need to explain the closet arrangement at my house. The secret to my marriage is quite simply his and hers closets. Through eleven years and three houses, my wife and I have each had our own closet. It's what keeps me out of trouble and my wife sane. My closet is my own personal sanctuary. It may be small and messy, but from this confined space, I transform every morning ready to take on the world, much like superman from his phone booth.

My closet is not tidy, but at least I know where everything is. Actually there are shirts I have not seen in years, but it is my mess. I can take comfort in its familiar surroundings. The bad weather, however, has brought out a mean streak in me. Maybe this time I can finally ditch that three-dollar clearance shirt that I have moved from house to house but never worn.

I started at the beginning. It didn't take long to empty the closet; it was putting it all back that was so daunting. I couldn't believe those heaps of clothes on the bed and floor had all fit in my closet just a few minutes ago.

The next task was to make a critical assessment of each item. This is where the ruthless part comes in. After a half hour and plenty of painful self-evaluation, I had a pile of five items I no longer needed. As coldblooded as I felt, this clearly was not enough. It was time to call in the big guns. Who is the one person you can count on to be utterly merciless about your clothes? That's right, your wife. Who better to tell you that your favorite t-shirt for the last twenty years would make great rags for cleaning the bathroom.

And ruthless she was. She coerced me into getting rid of the pair of shorts I always loved, but could no longer button. She convinced me that if I had not worn a shirt in the last five years, chances were slim I ever would. And if it wasn't blue, why bother keeping it at all? Blue is all I wear.

Three hours later, I was totally exhausted and had enough static electricity in my hair to light up the neighborhood. I thought we were almost done. All I had to do was pile everything back in the closet and close the door. It would not be that easy.

Once you get my wife started organizing, there is no off switch. This would have to run its course. She lives to organize. Her favorite part about going on vacation is packing for the trip.

I, on the other hand, am packing-averse and folding-impaired. I use a roll/fold/pile technique when putting clothes away. My wife beats the clothes into submission. She snaps the clothes with a rifle-loud crack, pinning the shoulders together, bending the arms and folding the body into a tightly-packed square.

Continuing her organizational rampage, my wife coordinated every piece of clothing based on color, type of fabric, and amount of use. My clothes were piled straighter than a Gap display before opening. I looked on in utter disbelief.

My closet was done, and I had to admit it never looked better. However, I was a little nervous about touching anything in fear that it would explode from its tightly-coiled position and bury me alive. But I could feel good about all the clothes I had to donate. I had found several new outfits I never knew I owned. And as an extra bonus, I entertained my wife for hours while replenishing our supply of bathroom cleaning rags.

It is always nice to reorganize, but it is a little like taking away superman's phone booth and giving him a cell phone. It may be more efficient, but we all need our own little space from which to take on the world.

- 2013 -

Transition Pieces

-tie one area of the puzzle to another-

As individuals we're just pieces of the community.

Alone we're misshapen bits, but together

we become something beautiful.

"Missing Pieces"

Sugar Pancakes

If we truly are what we eat, then my heart is made of sugar pancakes. On Saturday morning as kids, we'd have French pancakes, also known as crepes or what my family called sugar pancakes. Making them is an elaborate process of creating the perfect batter, cooking them just right and paper thin, quickly smothering them in butter and sugar, then rolling and cutting them in half while still piping hot. The downside is that only one can be made at a time, which exposed our family dynamics.

The four of us kids battled as each pancake was made, our mouths watering. The thought of someone else eating *our* pancake was unbearable.

My oldest sister played the martyr and deferred to her unsophisticated younger siblings in hopes that her sacrifice would be rewarded. But in the cut-throat world of sugar pancakes, it seldom was. She made her case for fairness and civility while pretending indifference. When all else failed, she called us immature and then created an alliance with me, using my status as the youngest to bolster her claim.

My second oldest sister was trickier. She tried to con our sugar pancakes from us. She once got me to do the dishes by pretending I was a robot boy, teaching me to move mechanically as I put away every dish and glass. Swindling my sugar pancake was child's play to her. I'm surprised she didn't have me serve it to her in bed as she pretended to be the Queen of England and I her trusty servant.

My brother, the third oldest, used brute force. He either pretended to spit on the sugar pancake or actually licked it to mark it as his own. That worked once or twice before Mom put a stop to it. He then shifted to a more subtle technique of describing every minor flaw as if the sugar pancake was a time bomb ready to explode, spraying the whole family with salmonella-like shrapnel. He of course threw himself on the pancake in true altruistic fashion.

Being the youngest, I had only one skill to call upon. I whined as only the youngest can. I complained of being picked on and, if all else failed, cried that the world was so unfair. To my surprise it usually worked and I got the very first sugar pancake. I should have known something was up.

It took me years to realize that the first sugar pancake is always the worst. It takes a couple of pancakes to get the pan temperature right and to tweak the thickness of the batter to achieve that delicate, delicious thinness. The fact that my second oldest sister bartered with me for the first pancake should have been a warning sign. She insisted the first pancake was the best, manipulating me to trade away my second and third for it. Oh, the horrors.

My parents were not immune to the power of the sugar pancake either. My Dad sat back and acted completely uninterested as if sugar pancakes were just like ordinary food. He waited patiently reading the paper and biding his time while we got full. Our interest waned as our bellies expanded until we were silent and satiated.

The pancakes kept coming and soon the oven was filled with ten perfect pancakes. My dad quietly ate every one of them in a Zen-like state while we kids watched in awe as butter dripped down his arm. We vowed to show such patience next time, but we never did. Who, after eating a sugar pancake, could blame us?

My mother turned out to be the most diabolical. I never saw her eat a single sugar pancake. She slaved at the stove, refusing all help. Her hands moved in a blur, pouring, flipping, buttering, sprinkling, rolling and cutting. She sacrificed so all of her children could bask in the glory of sugar pancakes.

It was only years later that she told me the truth. When she cut each pancake in half, my mother—the woman who would walk on glass for her children—ate the middle and most coveted part of each and every pancake. It's nice to know parents are human after all.

My parents are long gone now, and due to distance, I only see my siblings a few times a year. But I make sugar pancakes on a regular basis. When I miss a little of my youth or feel a hole where parents used to be, I start mixing the batter. I no longer have to fight over who gets the first sugar pancake, but some days, I wish I did.

- 2009 -

Missing Pieces

I grew up with an appreciation for jigsaw puzzles. My family would often work on a puzzle together, dispensing neighborhood gossip, news of relatives, and the occasional nugget of wisdom. We gathered around the table to observe and participate, like ancient tribes in years gone by. Through the philosophy of jigsaw puzzles we communicated the meaning of life using puzzle pieces as hieroglyphics to another world.

I'm currently working on a 750-piece puzzle featuring song birds. I start by separating all the edge pieces as my father taught me, putting together the borders to define the space. Then I start separating like-color pieces until I have honed it down to one unique shade as a place to begin. Using a combination of color and shape, I continue one piece at a time, filling in the cardinal, then the blue jay until all the birds are complete. I pick away at the transition pieces between bird and sky using the distinctive tap technique when necessary.

In my family, whenever anyone puts in a key piece that ties an element to the border, fills in a hole, or pioneers a new transition, they tap the piece to draw attention to their incredible accomplishment. The use of the tap is not regulated but rather dictated by the user's personality. My dad was a big tapper who further embellished the maneuver by calling it a coup.

In the last days of his life, my dad got the chance to do a lot of jigsaw puzzles and a lot of tapping. He was dying of pancreatic cancer. A unique thing about some cancers is their ability to tell time. My dad's prognosis was a year, and the cancer was very punctual. Near the end, as we cared for him in his home, cancer gave us twenty-eight days together, time to fit together a few more pieces and see the bigger picture.

We would work on jigsaw puzzles all day long and usually in the middle of the night. My dad believed if you didn't sleep you couldn't die, so at three in the morning we would be working on a jigsaw puzzle together. My dad worked on one section of the puzzle, trying to piece together the past, while I worked on another area, trying to find a transition piece between present and future.

So much of life was tied up in those pieces, as we struggled to fit together the bigger picture while examining each individual piece. We talked casually about shapes and colors, but perhaps more was said in the silent moments as we attempted to piece together the world.

Each puzzle piece is so much like a day. It's only a blurry bit of color until it's put into place and becomes a bird's eye or a section of fence. All the pieces scattered in different shapes and colors wait to be assembled into something meaningful. The days back then were blurry bits. Only later can those pieces be put together to make something to cherish.

I continue fitting pieces of my own life together, blurry day by blurry day. Some days I fill in a hole, finding the missing piece that has eluded me for so long. Other days I'm still working on my border. Most of the time I simply try to methodically work my way through the nondescript pieces looking for a message somewhere in the farm's field.

I try to get a glimpse of what my own jigsaw puzzle looks like, but there are still too many holes. I've completed sections here and there, but I'm still lacking some of those key transition pieces. My dad's jigsaw puzzle wisdom was to never look for any one piece for too long because some pieces never look like you think they should.

I remember many times looking for a woman's nose or a blue flag because they were so distinct. I picked up a piece with confidence only to realize I was mistaken. I tried every similar piece and finally quit in frustration. Only later when I wasn't looking for the woman's nose did it jump out at me, and I wondered how I could've missed it.

Another family tradition was to secretly hide a piece to be the last one to complete the puzzle. Two or three of us would be working on the few remaining pieces as the intensity picked up with limited choices. Sensing completion, the rest of my family would materialize each holding their own hidden piece, waiting to be last.

Some days it feels like I'm looking for hidden pieces—pieces my parents hold that I can no longer retrieve. Perhaps we're all hiding pieces of our own, wanting to hold back, fixating on a smudge of color and missing the larger canvas.

As individuals we're just pieces of the community. Alone we're misshapen bits, but together we become something beautiful. We race around trying to find where we belong. Some stand out like a cardinal's feather, but the majority of us have to find our place in the vast blue sky.

I enjoy jigsaw puzzles. I like looking for the bigger picture and finding meaning from seemingly unrelated pieces. Besides, sometimes when I'm focused on a puzzle, I might find myself in my father's living room and hear the distinct tap, tap, tap of a well-placed piece. What a coup indeed.

- 2010 -

Weatherman Jealousy

I'm jealous of the weatherman. He captivates my wife with his flashy graphics and colorful radar images. She hangs on his every word, making plans based on his advice. I become invisible, my ideas meaningless in the wake of all the meteorological gadgetry. It's not just one weatherman she's interested in, but a whole slew of local and national climate gigolos. The fact that some weathermen are women just confuses the issue even more.

I've gotten used to it—the late-night updates, the interrupted broadcasts, the quickly-muted weather forecast when I enter the room. I've learned to accept that my wife needs more weather information than I can provide by looking out the window. She's a planner and likes the illusion of control a weather report can provide. She understands the limitations of predicting the weather, but she wants the reassuring words like a bedtime story that allows us all to find some solace in this scary world so we can get some sleep.

My wife loves weather and thinks clouds are beautiful. She stares at weather maps, seeing something I don't. She listens to the forecast as if listening to a fortune teller. Her palm does look like the state of Wisconsin with her thumb becoming Door County. The weatherman traces the map, moving down her life-line and telling her future with enough detail to be engaging, yet with enough ambiguity to make it believable.

I take solace in knowing that with the internet she can get her weather fix without the weatherman. She watches radar maps as if a secret message is hidden in the colored blobs moving across the screen. She likes to decipher the raw data herself and is quite capable of reading the high temperatures listed on the map without being told. The problem is with greater access comes greater temptation. If we're going for a twenty-minute walk, my wife checks radar first and verifies pertinent data. Even if it's hot, humid, and miserable, she's happier knowing just how miserable it is.

When we go on a trip, my wife does research, studying weather forecasts for each possible location. I find it a little surreal. First, I don't like knowing the future any more than I have to, but knowing the future weather of a place I haven't even been to yet is just plain wrong. The weather is meant to be both powerful and mysterious. It's like trying to discover Superman's secret identity. Only bad things can happen.

The weatherman is a tease. Just when he's about to show tomorrow's forecast, he goes to a commercial. He hints at potentially dangerous storms that turn out to be not-so-treacherous later in the forecast. He strings my wife along with promises of information that never come and scares her with threats that never materialize. We're more gullible, trying to pacify our uneasiness with a force we can't control.

I personally don't like the weatherman. I secretly smile when he gets soaked by driving rain or pummeled in a blizzard during a forecast. He shows a map clearly displaying the temperatures of several cities, but still feels the need to read off each one as if translating Latin. He stands in front of the radar map blocking the view while telling me to watch the storm build. He says the same thing over and over again in a slightly different way in case I didn't know what the words *hot* and *humid* mean. Of course, I'm just jealous.

Weather is big in Wisconsin. It alters our mood and changes our lives. It's a predator we continually track, prowling the neighborhood, waiting to strike. We try to tame it with an extensive vocabulary and elaborate forecasts, but it won't be domesticated. Instead, we've made it into a god, worshiping it and weaving tales of its destructive powers. The weatherman becomes our spiritual leader in all things meteorological.

Unfortunately, the weatherman is mostly hype and a bit of a charlatan. He sensationalizes the weather and, by association, himself. Weather instruments boast aggressive military names and basic science is used as mystical powers kindly shared with us common folk. In a profession so often wrong, the weatherman exudes confidence and creativity, laying out a three-day forecast with such incredible hour-by-hour detail that it has to be true. It's not just going to rain tomorrow; it's going to rain at 9:43, and if it doesn't, all is forgotten like a politician's promise.

I've learned a few things over the years and have a solution. I bought my wife a home weather station with an anemometer for a gift. It sure beats the ant farm I gave her. I use words like dew point and barometric pressure on a daily basis, and when my wife asks about the weather, I make up a forecast so detailed and scientific that she hugs me for my enthusiasm, if not my accuracy. It just goes to show that even though the weather is uncontrollable, it's still a chick magnet.

- 2011 -

Fight or Flight

The human body is designed to deal with stress in one of two ways—fight or flight. We either stand and fight or flee and avoid. While this design was critical twelve thousand years ago, in today's society punching the boss or hiding from housework is counter-productive. So how do we deal with our Neanderthal DNA in this more subtle world? Running is the answer.

Running allows us to exercise both fight and flight. In a world where we get our exercise from Wii Fit, form relationships virtually online, and debate our greatest issues in silent tweets, we need at least one connection to our more primitive self. Running allows us the opportunity to escape maybe not a woolly mammoth, but heart disease and diabetes, and to fight off the boredom of our sedentary lives.

The fight begins in the early morning when we barely have the strength to open our eyes or the flexibility to tie our shoes. Yet somehow, we battle through a million excuses just to get out of bed. As if the mental jousting were not enough, we make it out the door before daybreak, and begin to move faster than we will all day.

The fight is ongoing and completely internal—I'm not a runner, I'm too tired, too slow. We battle self-doubt, we sink our teeth into hesitation, we rip apart stereotypes that contain us. When confronted with forces that limit us, we beat them back by the simple act of getting out of bed, putting on our shoes, and moving one foot in front of the other.

We continue to challenge ourselves by entering races. We line up with little more than a pair of shoes to do battle for miles. In herd-like fashion we roam the hills and plains knowing instinctively the weakest and slowest are the first to fall prey. We battle not for placement—whether we come in 878th or 879th makes little difference—but we push for a desire to know ourselves. We seek to find the edges of our capabilities and extrapolate who we are. In the end, we cross the finish line alone and seek our own meaning to the struggle

Running is also the greatest example of flight. In the most basic sense. We run away from conflict. While the battle is invigorating, escape is even more rewarding. There can be no more calming experience than running away from confusion, running away from guilt, running away from all the little messages telling us we're not good enough.

Running is an opportunity to leave it all behind, shut off the brain and experience what's really tangible. Concentrate on the breath, experience our body in motion, float on the rhythms of the earth. Running isn't so much about running away from problems as it is running to a sense of calm.

Celebrate the accomplishment. On days when it seems I can accomplish nothing, I secretly smile knowing I ran six miles. I moved forward in a very real and physical way. I kept my body healthy, my mind free, and my soul cleansed.

Running can simply be fun. It's the closest we can come to flying on our own power. We celebrate the kid inside us all as we zoom across the ground with the wind in our hair and our cape flapping in the breeze. Nobody wears a cape to stand still. We want to soar.

We didn't call it running when I was a kid. We called it playing and, in typical kid fashion, the faster you went the more it felt like flying. We never ran in a straight line, but zigzagged through the neighborhood, living a million adventures in a single afternoon.

I'm a runner. I do it for many reasons. Every time I feel the urge to fight when someone cuts me off or flee when asked to clean the bathroom, I feel my life get slightly out of balance. I run and literally exercise my instincts back into harmony.

So, if you find yourself listing to the right from overusing the remote control or feel that general unease for reasons unknown, maybe it's time to give running a try. It's not about how fast you go; it's about finding balance in a world that is slightly out of step.

- 2009 -

Trust at the Grocery Store

I was shopping at the grocery store the other day when I noticed a woman. Actually I noticed her purse, sitting wide open in her grocery cart. She had her back turned and was ten feet away from her cart, examining produce. My emotions started with guilt, ran to suspicion, and moved on to encouragement, contentment, and finally alarm. All of this from a purse. Grocery shopping can be a nightmare.

When I first saw the vulnerable purse, I felt guilty for noticing it. Perhaps just looking would turn me into a criminal. I must have something wrong with me for noticing her purse unless I was planning on stealing it. I should have just told her to keep her purse in her possession at all times, but how guilty would that look? The SWAT team would burst out of the neatly stacked lettuce and subdue me instantly. I needed to move on.

As I started towards the bakery, another thought hit me. Someone must protect this woman and her purse from the inevitable hordes of purse pilferers in the store. Everyone knows you are not supposed to leave your valuables unguarded. I thought of throwing myself on the purse to protect it, but I didn't want to create a scene. After all, I was here to pick up a few groceries, not be a hero. But the task had fallen to me and I was not about to let this shopper or her purse down.

I watched from a distance, analyzing every customer for criminal intent. Was that man really looking at the oranges or scoping out his prey? I had pegged three separate people as homicidal maniacs or at least produce abusers. One was eating grapes he had not purchased, another was over-handling the apples, and the third was mangling the lettuce. All criminals need to start somewhere. First, they abuse the produce and then they snatch a purse. Who knows, maybe they'd steal a car in the parking lot on their way out.

After several minutes without a single handbag abduction, I was encouraged—a woman felt safe enough to leave her purse unguarded. If she could let her guard down, so could I. Apparently every other person in the store was not a criminal but actually there to buy groceries. I noticed several purses equally unguarded, and I had to conclude that people were generally trusting and equally trustworthy.

My simple stop at the grocery store turned into an epiphany. The world was a much better place than I had heard on TV. We could be trusted—I could be trusted. We're basically safe, danger does not lurk around every corner, and, except for some abused produce, people are pretty decent. I didn't need to worry anymore; everything would work out fine.

Then it hit me—we feel too content. We are not on our guard enough. First, we trust strangers in the store, then we start believing what we hear on the news, next we trust CEOs, and finally we fall for what the politicians are shoveling. Like a teenager blissfully disengaged, we feel untouchable knowing someone else will clean up the mess and make things right. We stop protecting our environment, our children's education, our grandchildren's future, our basic human rights.

We trust someone is looking out for our best interests. We don't need to vote or know the issues. We don't need to protest or praise or doubt because someone else will do that for us. Buy the cheapest everything and trust the jobs will remain. Pretend our food is safe when we don't recognize the ingredients on the label. Let our politicians be bought and sold by corporations. Someone out there will make sure it all turns out right.

While I could watch over this one women's purse for an afternoon, I had no plan for the rest of the world. I finally realized that maybe we should take turns watching out for each other. When my back is turned, hopefully someone will keep watch. The only problem is that we all see danger differently, which might explain why the woman hit me when I tried to rescue her from the fluorescent Pop-Tarts wedged into her cart.

Try as I might, I can no more save anyone as I can condemn them. I left the grocery store that day not gripping my billfold, but clutching my heart. Maybe we work too hard to protect material things while everything of real meaning is left up for grabs.

- 2005 -

Afternoon Adventures

I need an adventure. As a kid, adventures were an everyday occurrence that required minimal planning for maximum entertainment. A canteen and enough trees to block out civilization were all I needed to battle aliens, glimpse Bigfoot, or find secret hideouts. But it's not the discoveries I miss: it's the exploration. I want the wonderment that comes from the first walk on the moon, leaping from bed to bed. I might be older, but it's time for an adventure.

I used to traverse the globe in my living room with little cars, pieces of cut-up fabric as sleeping bags, and snacks for both pretend and real explorers. I'd maneuver my car with its neatly packed supplies through the shag carpet and up the arm of the couch. Sometimes it took hours to cross the world and other times only fifteen minutes, with me making car revving noises the whole way—va-room, va-room. I saw incredible sights and made harrowing escapes with tires screeching and wheels spinning.

Now I drive a much bigger car with greater technology, more cargo space, ample cup holders, and a real engine, but I don't travel nearly as far. When I drive today I still make cool screeching sounds as I round corners, but I'm generally just getting from point A to point B. Though my car now has more horsepower, it lacks the imaginary drive to go cross-country in an afternoon. As I get older, it's harder to find cars that run on pretend gas, and with pretend gas prices through the roof, travel becomes more difficult. Pretend money doesn't grow on trees. Elves make it.

An adventure is all about the journey—jumping on furniture to avoid the lava flow or scaling the stairway with ropes and footholds because it's there. The destination is meaningless and comes with the risk of turning an adventure into a *trip* that requires photos and a t-shirt just to remember the experience. The best adventures go nowhere, allowing us to enter a much bigger world of possibilities.

Adventures are not tasks to complete. In a good adventure, the quest changes with the mood. Checking items off a to-do list fills us with a sense of purpose and accomplishment, but a good adventure infuses us with wonder and delight. Between vacuuming and dusting, why not look for a secret passageway that leads to the experimental laboratory. Every house has one and very few people ever find it.

Adventures teach us to be forgiving of ourselves and others. As all good explorers know, mistakes are inevitable. When the spaceship Kenmore starts veering left, it's impossible to know the exact purpose for each dial and knob since we drew them on the cardboard box only an hour ago. Under pressure of crashing on the moon, action must be taken. It's not about being right, but being miserably wrong and somehow still righting the ship.

We're afraid of being wrong. We have to know all the answers before we begin. We'll never come to understand any idea like an adventurer who braves the unknown, makes decisions on the fly, and learns by doing rather than listening to someone else explain how it's done.

It's impossible to develop really great ideas without the possibility of coming up with equally bad ones. The adventurer is willing to take that risk and explore each idea without fear. Every idea is another adventure filled with the excitement of new discoveries, like the time I tried to invent a new beverage at age ten by mixing every liquid I could find in the refrigerator. I'm not sure pickle juice with milk was a good idea.

Life is meant to be an adventure, not a chore. We're supposed to be dramatic and playful. We were meant to explore and be curious, but we've become so cautious. I was never good at completing the Rubik's Cube. The only way to complete the puzzle was by disturbing one of the already completed sides, and I was afraid I'd lose the progress I'd made. The same fear happens in life. The more we have, the less we risk until we are in complete maintenance mode, unable to solve new problems.

We need to find adventure as we get older and no longer fit in the washing machine box. We need to risk, explore new concepts, and tap into the mind of a child, where digging a hole to China is possible. To truly grow as individuals, we need to act like a child and sit on the roof for no better reason than to get a new perspective. I have to go now. The elves are here with more pretend money.

- 2012 -

Small Talk

Few people know me and I'm the only one to blame. I don't converse, preferring instead to debate the nuances of some obscure point of view. I can talk about feelings and possibly gardening. I just have no way to get from hello to the middle of a great conversation. I've never mastered the art of small talk. I grew up discussing the meaning of life and why we exist. I'm used to being blunt and philosophical, not delightful and entertaining.

I always thought small talk had no purpose. I was wrong. It's the snack that tides us over until dinner. That quick smile and friendly word keeps us satisfied until the bigger issues kick in. I still hesitate, not sure what to say, like being hungry but not knowing what to eat. I just stand with the refrigerator door open, unable to relate to the carton of eggs. I'm the same with people, never knowing where to begin. Asking if they think we exist to experience life or achieve goals doesn't seem appropriate.

Once contact has been made, silence becomes deadly. My brain goes through a progression of possible openings, finding flaws with each until finally going to my safety-valve topic: the weather. Once snowfall counts are totaled, my brain goes numb. I feel myself float away as my last thread to humanity is severed, at least until another conversational line can be secured to keep me hanging by a thread.

I see people I know, but then pretend I don't. It's not that I want to avoid them. I'm afraid. It's the fear of silence and the small talk required to avoid it. I don't have anything interesting to say and talking about nothing depresses me. Maybe I'm expecting too much and fail to see all the other threads connecting us in so many ways, or I'm buried in my own little world and can't get free. It's easier to duck.

Partly it's a guy thing. Not that guys can't talk about feelings or be emotional; it just takes us longer to get there. Topics are limited to sports, cars, beer, movies and TV, or work. Motorcycles can be substituted for cars, and fishing can count as a sport even if it's more of a recreational hobby. Wine can take the place of beer, but only if a woman is present, while substituting music or books for movies is not allowed. The rules are daunting and leave little room for in-depth conversations, but I have missed the point again.

Small talk is the doorway to bigger conversations, with a bouncer checking IDs and keeping out the riff-raff. We start with football, looking for compatibility. If the Bears get mentioned in a positive way, we back off slowly, and then run like hell. Only when we find some connection on at least three of the five categories do we begin to discuss the bigger topics of food, hobbies, and lawn care. After about ten years of successful exchange, the conversation might get into the heavier subjects of spiritual beliefs, dreams, and prostate issues.

Small talk only goes so far. Good conversation requires a connection, an investment of resources. Words need to be followed by emotions and actions, which means taking risks. Here's where I fail. I want to connect, but when I finally reach out, I realize I don't really have the other people's attention or their response is a trick, designed to persuade not engage. I become overwhelmed and start pulling back, closing my eyes, plugging my ears, and humming a catchy tune.

While I block out conversations, others insulate themselves with technology. Messages are sent via Facebook and texted from the safety of our own private worlds. When walking out in public, eye contact is avoided to minimize exposure of an impromptu encounter. Soon we're alone.

I was never good at polite conversation. It's a long journey, one I'm seldom patient enough to make. I look for short cuts, but none exist. Yet without the initial investment, I get no closer to making lasting connections. I could blame my lack of effort on external forces, but that would be misplaced criticism. I need to make an attempt with a simple hello, not so much as a conversation starter, but as a wakeup call to me: to be connected, one has to connect. If that fails—how about those Packers?

- 2012 -

Distinct Pieces

-stand out but don't look like what we expect-

Our experience is limited by our ability to perceive,

not the world's capacity to share. What we care to notice,

what we dare to see, defines not our path,

but our experience.

"Distance Matters"

Confessions of a Saver

I must confess—I've been a bad consumer. I haven't used much gas, eaten out enough, or bought many clothes. I haven't even purchased a smart TV. I'm still a big spender compared to people in most other countries, but here in the USA I'm a dismal failure. Part of this country's financial disaster is my fault. Since responsibility is the buzz word, I take full responsibility for my poor purchasing prowess.

It isn't as if I didn't try. I bought things I didn't need, even frivolous things. I bought more groceries than I could eat and threw some away. I bought a DVD because I felt like it. I bought a pair of pants that I only wore once and will probably never wear again. I paid homage to the marketers, buying things I didn't even know I needed.

My problem is, I'm a saver. There, I said it. My name is Christopher Kunz and I'm a saver. I know the first step is being able to admit it. I like to save money. I like the sense of security it gives me, however false, and I'm fascinated by the concept of compound interest.

It started with my first savings account at age twelve. I watched $20 grow to $20.84. I was hooked. I started experimenting with money markets, CDs, and mutual funds, finally graduating to stocks and bonds. Now I'm in withdrawal, my supply dried up. The market has disowned me, disregarding all that I've done for it.

My mother was a spender. She knew you couldn't take it with you, and she was right. She didn't give big tips—she gave outrageous tips. She bought locally and sought quality. She loved to find deals and treated flea markets like a treasure hunt. She gave generously to charities, believing that money given freely would always come back to you. She didn't spend what she didn't have, but when she had it, she spent it with a passion, enjoying every moment.

I worry about money: not having enough and asking for help, or having too much while others have so little. I worry about spending wisely and investing soundly. I buy items, then worry if I got the best price. I contemplate the stock market's theoretical concept of money and mourn the dollars lost in my battle for financial independence.

Like a typical commitment-fearing male, I'm afraid of credit and the future debt it implies. In today's society, credit is a necessity for starting a business or buying anything larger than a bicycle, but it comes with a heavy weight. Instead of being a liberator, credit can become a jailer, creating a ten-year sentence of hard labor to pay for the last remodeling project.

Unfortunately, our economy is influenced so heavily by our own consumption that the advice most often heard is spend, spend, spend—stockpile more collectibles, go further into debt. Our jobs depend on us spending beyond our means, creating an unsustainable financial model.

At least we can take pride in the fact that our purchasing power drives this country and many others. With pressure to keep up, I do feel inadequate in my spending. Bigger homes, bigger cars, and a never-ending supply of electronic gadgets keep our economy going and my head spinning.

I struggle with what is enough. How much money do I need to feel safe? How many gadgets should I own to be happy? How much do I give away to feel peace? I try to strike a balance, but I feel the ground has shifted under my feet. What was enough ten years ago falls far short today.

My TV is over ten years old, meaning I'm at least three upgrades behind and two sizes too small. It doesn't matter that my old TV still works great. How could I deny myself all the features now available, even if I don't understand what most of those features do? Still, I hang on knowing happiness is not tied to the TV, but in choosing it for the right reasons.

As a country we work more hours, take on more stress, and see each other less. We put our health at risk and strain relationships in an attempt to pay for the two-year-old car, last year's vacation, last month's cable bill, and yesterday's double mochaccino with a half pump of hazelnut.

For those few enlightened people like my mother who see the mystical loop of the dollar, money will never own them. For the savers and worriers like me, money will always involve a love/hate relationship. For the spenders in all of us, remember that ownership is an illusion, good health trumps everything, and family and friends are the only true currency.

- 2009 -

First Day of School

I'm a little sad when school starts. I'm jealous I'm not going. I always liked school, and I start feeling left out when I see the back-to-school displays and realize I won't be getting any new notebooks or a new sixty-four pack of crayons with its own sharpener. No new school outfits for me.

I can still smell the change in the air and the excitement of new beginnings. I liked the first day of school the best—no homework due, no expectations to fulfill. It's like one big party as you meet old friends you haven't seen all summer and search for new classrooms as if you were on a treasure hunt. Pencils still have their erasers and that carefree attitude of summer lingers in the hallways.

Each new teacher is a possible genius/mentor/educator extraordinaire and each classmate a potential new best friend. It's only later we find out our teacher listens to Pat Boone and has worn the same outfit since the very first day. Our potential new best friend is that one weird kid who inexplicably eats the paste. But on that first day with the energy buzzing and nearly anything possible, I feel the most alive.

Even after the first day rush, and long after the monotony has set in, school still offers up endless treasures. I remember Ms. Metcalf, my sixth-grade math teacher. We called her *Ms.* That was a new thing in my school roughly thirty-five years ago; we called female teachers *Ms.* I loved it.

I never understood the *Mrs.* and *Miss* or how you pronounced them. One meant you were married and the other didn't, but I could never remember which was which—as if teachers were allowed to have a life outside of school in the first place, not to mention be married. And somehow at the age of twelve, I was supposed to understand the difference? *Ms.* was a gift.

Ms. Metcalf made math fun through her sheer excitement and great teaching style. I still remember improper fractions to this day because of her. She called them Raquel Welch fractions because they were top heavy. After boring years of multiplication tables and long division, I was given Raquel Welch fractions and excelled at math throughout my remaining school years.

My fifth-grade homeroom teacher, Ms. Miller, made me a Christmas stocking of felt, sewn together and decorated with my nickname spelled in shiny little disks. It had a small pocket on the front where she put a candy cane and hung it on the wall with the other twenty-eight stockings.

I still have mine after all these years and put it on our Christmas tree every year, partly because it's cute and partly because it's a treasure. It represents all the little treasures remembered and forgotten through the many school years.

I had my share of anxieties too—riding the bus for the first time, taking a shower after gym, and reading out loud in class. I had braces, cowlicks and a really long awkward stage, but I was having too much fun to notice. As years soften the memories, even the traumatic moments become treasured learning experiences.

Like the time I argued against the whole class, including the teacher, about the word *impossible*. We were learning the difference between *improbable* and *impossible*, when I said, "well, something can be improbable, but not impossible." Mayhem ensued as I rattled off increasingly creative responses to every impossible thing they could think of.

"It is impossible for you to fly on your own power," came the challenge. I reasonably explained that perhaps I was from outer space and unbeknownst to them I could indeed fly. The teacher finally gave up in frustration, and I never felt so strongly that anything was possible.

It is that same feeling today that makes me envious of all the students heading off to school. Anything is possible. While it is improbable any of your classmates are from outer space, it's very possible that one of them could be a dear and close friend decades later.

So when the September winds kick up the chalkboard dust and schools open their doors, embrace the possibilities. Public school offers the best smorgasbord in town. Hopes and dreams along with fears and anxieties swirl around, creating every opportunity in the world. Enjoy your first day both students and teachers alike. Those notebooks and crayons won't be new forever.

- 2009 -

Flex Your Superpowers

I always wished I had special powers. Maybe I could be a genius with numbers, read minds, or fly. There's a certain confidence that comes with knowing you're a man of steel. I wouldn't just be a hero. I'd be a superhero. I would fear nothing and be admired for saving the world.

But special powers are hard to come by. If I was born on Krypton I might stand a chance, but I've never even been to Europe. There is no pill to take (unless you're Underdog) or class to enroll in, although there are people who would have you believe so. We are stuck with who we are and our ordinary run-of-the-mill abilities.

As it turns out, those abilities are all it takes. I don't want to sound corny, but to my friends and family I have special powers. My achievements, while small in comparison to Einstein, Aquaman, or Harry Potter, are greeted with fanfare and encouragement. I'm not a superhero, I'm just super lucky. My wife has seen me at my worst, yet she is my biggest fan and I can't even deflect bullets.

I am no genius, but I can balance the checkbook. I can't fly, but I did finish several marathons. I can't read minds, but I am always trying to figure out what my wife is thinking. And I certainly don't have super human strength, but I have been known to open really tight jar lids from time to time.

Just the other day I parallel parked with such precision and speed it was poetry in motion. When I dug up some shrubs along the driveway, I tore them apart. I can dig like nobody's business. I took on three spiders single-handedly with just a stick. These were big spiders too, with genetically-enhanced qualities. I can also cook a pretty mean salmon patty, but I am not expecting media coverage or my own TV series. I get a grin from my wife and that's enough.

So, step aside Superman, Wonder Woman, and Spidey. You might be able to save the world from mutant creatures with laser-beam eyes, but can you scrape three layers of paint off an antique table without scratching it? I didn't think so.

We are surrounded by superheroes who just lack marketing and spin. If teachers got the same press as Harry Potter, we would finally appreciate the magic they perform every day in the classroom. I know many of them wear glasses.

If administrative assistants had their own comic strip, we might finally understand how they save the day time after time. Imagine Super Sharon using her lightning speed and mind-reading capabilities to discover the elusive document and save the company once again.

If nurses had their own fan club, we would be more interested in how many lives they touched each day. We would line the parking lot and scream for their autographs. Bright purple and green pajama-like outfits would be the fashion rage as we all tried to emulate our favorite heroes.

Why do we celebrate someone who can throw a football instead of someone who can throw together a fabulous meal? There is something special about good food and the people who can make it. Try eating a football sometime. Every day the world is filled with people simply doing what needs to be done. These everyday acts go unnoticed by the vast majority, but I imagine, or at least hope, that someone special is there to celebrate each of these small victories.

We may not climb Mt. Everest or get in the Guinness Book of World Records, but we make a difference to the people around us. We are just too busy rooting for the home team to realize we *are* the home team. Raising kids, taking care of parents, helping a neighbor, volunteering—these are the things that make us successful. Forget about trying to fly and figure out how to brighten the lives of those that mean the most to us.

Being a superhero really wouldn't make me any happier. I would get a cape—which is pretty cool—but I wouldn't make my wife smile any brighter than if I cleaned the bathroom. Besides, the tights have a tendency to creep up on a person, and who needs that.

- 2010 -

The Unknown

We will die. We will be dead for a long time. Those are the facts. But death often remains just beyond our mental field of vision, an outcome too removed to comprehend while there are dishes to do and bills to pay. When I was diagnosed with stage IV colon cancer, death loomed much closer. As I approach death, I get no greater insight, only a desire to incorporate death into my world view.

I imagine death as a form of the big bang, but as my own fun-sized version where death constricts my soul, making it so dense it explodes and showers my annoying habit of asking "why?" into the cosmos. Blissfully, I don't know what happens when I die. One of the fears of death is the unknown, but this lack of knowledge is also invigorating. If we knew what happens when we die, we would spend all of our lives preparing for it. We are distracted enough as it is.

I take solace in the ambiguity of death. Whether death is one big party or a timeless dimensional shift or a peek behind the universe, I will never know, not while I'm alive. There's a reason we love mysteries. They compel us, drive us forward. We want to see over the next ridge, find out whodunit, understand the cosmos. We seek to look beyond ourselves. The unknown should not scare as much as fascinate us.

I want to be fascinated, but I'm staring at the end of something beautiful—my life—where I no longer exist. I'm interested in where I'm going next, but I'm still trying to wrap my head around where I've been. What becomes of my dreams, those fulfilled and the ones still out there? I have never been interested in leaving a mark on this world. It's been marked up plenty. I do, however, want to examine my life, not to judge it, but to understand if any part of it is transferable.

I cry more easily now, and more often—watching a movie, thinking about a moment—not because I'm sad, but because I'm moved. I'm moved by life's beauty—the taste of a hot fudge sundae, the hum of a party, the feel of my wife's body against mine in a hug. These sensations haven't changed. I have. I focus inwardly, cramming events into my life of experiences to see where they will fit, trying to patch holes and strengthen walls.

Each experience brightens when viewed through the lens of finality. I think of each moment as possibly my last—my last annual pizza party, my last Christmas—and I'm compelled to hold on to these experiences longer, afraid to set them down and lose them forever. I find myself slowly saying goodbye to pieces of my life, like thinning possessions in the house so when I finally move, I won't be overwhelmed.

I think about the past more, about friends I have not seen in years or decades. I can envision my timeline from beginning to end as I gather up moments, relive parties, and replay conversations, studying them as works of art. I want to unfurl these gorgeous moments and breathe in the beauty of each word spoken, every connection made. I re-play these moments not merely to remember, but to strengthen my soul for its new beginning.

I don't know what happens when we die. The unknown has transported us beyond the moon. The mysterious fuels our imaginations and pushes us to understand what the generation before us did not. People talk about faith. To me, faith is embracing the unknown without dogma or certainty, stepping boldly forward, opening to all possibilities.

So if you find yourself pondering some obscure notion or craving chocolate or needing to build a snowman, know it is me exploding through your personal cosmos, scattering the essence of what it was to be me.

- 2020 -

Distance Matters

Distance matters. I live a small life, measured in feet instead of miles. I'm forty-five hundred feet from downtown and the library, less than fifteen hundred feet from two parks, a museum, and a lake. These easily walkable and bikeable distances allow me a more intimate relationship with my community where weather plays a bigger role and each outing is personal.

If I lived farther from these places I wouldn't visit them as often. I might think I would, but distance has a convenience threshold that's hard to overcome in a car. Certain obligations must be met to drive, requiring a driver's license, glasses, and locating keys. These tasks create a barrier which casual trips cannot break.

Shorter distances mean we live closer together, our lives more transparent. We can see this as a limitation with less control, but I see community as family with shared experiences, an intimate loss of privacy, and intrinsic trust that comes from seeing the same people every day. Neighbors become an extension of our family, crazy uncles and all.

Maneuvering in this kind of community requires honesty. As the space between us shrinks, we become more exposed. We risk conversations along our path. We become victim to the elements. We can't rely on a simple finger wave through our windshield. We must engage, never sure what turn life will take, when a pleasant greeting will morph into a confessional or a quick walk will become a three-hour event.

This closeness fosters a web of connections, linking us together. Our waiter could also be a farmer we buy vegetables from at the farmer's market. Our neighbor might be our child's teacher or a local business owner or the person approving our car loan. Everyone must be treated kindly because we never know when the person ringing up our groceries might also be the volunteer we need at our next fundraising event or the parent of our child's new best friend.

Shorter distances don't mean my world is getting smaller, only richer. Experiences calibrate to fit the distance. A walk to the library on a snowy day has as many surprising elements as a drive a thousand times longer. Our experience is limited by our ability to perceive, not the world's capacity to share. What we care to notice, what we dare to see, defines not our path, but our experience.

Place matters. The French have a word for it—*terroir*—referring to grapes mostly, meaning that the soil, altitude, and weather from a particular location impart their characteristics on the grapes, yielding distinct qualities. We are at least as susceptible as grapes to our surroundings.

We take in energy from downtown, calmness from trees lining the streets. The lake exposes an expansive horizon, revealing the earth's vulnerabilities, making ours seem small in comparison. Schools give us hope like small power plants, producing curiosity and pumping it directly into the community. We bathe in the sound of kids playing at the city pool and seldom realize the impact these simple elements have on our lives.

My community holds me together, ties me to reality. When I travel away from home, I flail, looking for something to hold on to. I lack place and feel distorted by distance, as anxious as the changing landscape flashing by. Even when I stop moving, I'm lost, my identity left back at home. As nice as it is to step outside myself, soon I yearn for my foundation, my touchstone.

I haven't always lived where I do today, just as I'm not the same person I was thirty years ago. We search for place, an identity, somewhere we belong, and if we're lucky we also find ourselves along the way. I'm finally in synch with my community, folded into the city's collective breath. This connection gives me peace and a space to practice being me.

Place is part of who we are as we pick up small idiosyncrasies like grapevines absorb minerals. Finding where we grow best is essential and defined partly by distance. The more in tune we are with our location, the closer we want to be to its heartbeat. Have you hugged your community lately?

- 2015 -

Cooking with Joy

I like to cook. I like the creative process, the experimentation, and the tasty results. My mom taught me to be fearless in the kitchen as she threw in a handful of spices and used up leftover wine. From seemingly unrelated ingredients and a little knowledge, I can make a meal that not only feeds a hunger, but starts conversations and creates emotions.

Cooking sets you free. If your wife's specialties are popcorn and toast, have no fear: your options are endless. If you have a craving for French toast at two in the morning, no sweat. Even when you have nothing in the pantry except olive oil and garlic, you can still eat like royalty.

Food is a fabulous thing. It comes in bright colors, with tantalizing smells, primeval textures, and flavors that unlock the subconscious. While we've learned to do horrific things to our food by creating things like cheeseburger-flavored potato chips and s'more cereal, we also have the power within us to take basic ingredients and create a vegetable soup so good and healthy we could be accused of healthcare reform.

Just shopping for ingredients can be exhilarating. The farmer's market is filled with interesting food and people. Recipes and cooking advice can be found as easily as heirloom tomatoes and eggplant. Food is treated as treasure, dug up, cleaned, and counted like gold doubloons.

When I go into Jacob's Meat Market, I'm like a kid in a candy store. I stare at the meat cases, looking at all the options and weighing out possibilities. Only a nudge from my wife wakes me from my trance. I look for the right sausage for a black bean soup and leave with an armful of a treats.

I'd like to be a vegetarian, especially since I know what happens in the name of inexpensive grocery store meat, but food is a funny thing. Intertwined through birthday parties, holiday gatherings, and romantic dinners, food creates a series of emotional triggers. We are what we eat, but what we choose to eat is affected by who we last ate a particular meal with and how we celebrated. The rational part of our brain doesn't stand a chance.

My mom was almost always disappointed with food at restaurants. She would say the food was bland or the preparation flawed, but what I think she sensed was the lack of emotional involvement with the food. While others might appreciate a French dip, my mother could detect the laziness in the sodium-packed au jus.

When she found a restaurant and a meal she liked, it was a party. The unspoken rule was that nobody could order the same thing and everyone had to share. It was as if six people combined into one, with the food connecting us all in an invisible vortex of bliss. All barriers were dropped and communication became an involuntary reaction, causing me to tell my whole family the details of prom night.

Food can transport us to places that can't be reached any other way. From our own kitchens, we can visit any country with the right spices, create any atmosphere with the proper ingredients, and transcend time with enough care. Having a wonderful meal at Cannova's, with the lively conversation and music in the background, feels more like being in Italy than eating a Big Mac in Rome. Food is the universal language and cooking is how we communicate.

When each sibling reached the age of food awareness, we were awarded a cookbook filled with Mom's recipes, handwritten in large cursive and steeped in mystery. She didn't own a measuring cup or spoon, so each recipe's measurements had to be translated from the original white coffee cup and bent spoon.

None of the recipes can be taken literally either. You need to compensate for mood, selective memory, and attitude. When making her simple five-ingredient brownies, first you need to reduce the oil from one coffee cup to three-quarters of a measuring cup, and even less if you're in a health-conscious mood. Don't forget the vanilla. Even though it's not in the recipe, it's implied. Finally, add a splash of coffee if you're feeling adventurous.

When I get together with my sisters, we cook. We cram into small kitchens and try to impress each other with our latest discoveries. The kitchen quickly takes on a carnival atmosphere with knifes flying and water boiling as we each elbow for more stage. Even when we're not together, we call to regale each other with our latest culinary success.

I learned to cook by being in the kitchen while my mom made potato pancakes black with pepper or her incredible pea soup with whole yellow peas. She taught me an appreciation for food and that life, like cooking, doesn't follow any perfect recipe. The joy comes from always trying to make it a little bit better.

- 2011 -

Fear of Loneliness

I'm afraid of many things. I wish I weren't. I make some decisions out of fear and pretend it's logic. I worry about outcomes that will never happen, and react to threats that aren't there. I'm afraid of situations that, on closer inspection, shouldn't be scary. It's not that I'm a fearful person, just someone with too much to lose and an overactive imagination where anything is possible.

I can only admit this on the eve of the Summer Solstice, when the days are longest and the nights are short and mild, emboldening me with a false sense of security. Even with the windows open to the outside world, the cricket's familiar song fills me with hope and a peaceful night's sleep.

As a kid I used to sing out loud when I went down to the basement alone, thinking that if my family heard me suddenly stop singing, they would know I was being attacked and come to my rescue. I also thought my singing would warn any monsters of my presence so they could hide before I saw them. If I was being more discreet, I would talk to myself or clomp my feet extra loud, just so I couldn't hear hairy beasts whispering clandestine plans or slimy creatures slipping back into the crevices from which they came.

Not much has changed in the last forty years. I've just become more subtle, applying the same tactics to everyday life. I continue to make noise, hoping to drown out the sound of critics, reminding people around me that I'm still alive. The monsters haven't changed much either. The scariest ones are creatures I can't see, so naturally I imagine their fangs longer, their claws sharper, their stature bigger. No monster exists that is scarier than my own imagination.

I'm afraid of more than monsters. Sometimes a simple word is terrifying. *No* is a tiny word, but more ferocious than the biggest beast. Alone on the page or uttered without context, *no* isn't frightening, like a room of friends in the daylight. Only when it's creeping around a request or favor asked does its presence become eerie, waiting until I'm at my most vulnerable before attacking my pride, stabbing my dignity multiple times.

I do most of my own damage before *no* can sink its teeth into me by declining to make a request, thinking the worst no matter how unrealistic it might be, to the point where *no* doesn't even have to make an appearance. I'm frightened by the knowledge that it exists, like terrorists and Ebola, where the thought is worse than the word itself because the idea is always present, lurking in the back of my mind.

When I'm home alone I'm scared of intruders, placing my cell phone near my bed, imagining someone cutting the phone lines as I double check that all the doors are locked. In bed, each creak represents an armed prowler who has come to steal my antique malt mixer and vintage Happy Days lunch box. I debate if I should cough to make noise, scaring them off before they enter my bedroom with loaded AK-47s or if I should remain quiet, hoping they will just leave.

When my petite five-foot-two-inch wife with no martial arts skills is home, I'm content. It's not that I think my wife can protect me from an intruder, but as it turns out, she can save me from myself.

I think differently when I'm alone, spending more time contemplating life and connecting with feelings that I don't examine at other times. This introspection can be a good thing, but turned on its side it can create fear, longing, and a compulsive need to replay events like a teenager listening to a new song over and over until what was once beautiful becomes annoying.

My wife keeps me company. Sometimes we'll be in different rooms and won't have spoken to each other in hours, but I know she's there and that makes all the difference. The six-headed beast with fists like boulders and a spiny tail is no match for my wife. She can easily take him out with just a smile.

Whether confronting a fifty-foot monster or a two-letter word or things that go bump in the night, the answer isn't stronger doors and higher fences, but more friends and deeper connections. Because if we wall ourselves off, we're left with the worst monster of all: loneliness.

Wait, did you hear that?

- 2013 -

Odd-Shaped Pieces

-stand out for their form more than their image-

Life takes a certain amount of patience

to truly enjoy. We need time to catch our breath,

notice a sunset, listen to our own heart

beat that magical rhythm.

"The Breath of Life"

Mom's Magazines

My mom sent me another magazine today. She does that periodically. I'm never sure what the magazine is going to be or even when I will get it, but it's always a nice surprise. It is almost as if my mom knows what I need before I do. What makes these magazine deliveries even more amazing is that my mom has been dead for several years.

The idea of someone watching over me was always a vague and somewhat soothing notion. After my mom died, it felt much more personal and intimidating. Now my mom can see everything I think and do. As if she didn't already have an uncanny ability to know everything about my life when she was alive, now I don't stand a chance of keeping any secrets.

It's her continual ability to make an impact that's so amazing. Recently I talked of going to Italy even though I am not a big traveler. The next week I received a travel magazine with a cover story about Italy. Even more eerie, the story was about a mother and son bike trip. She used to work her magic with a few phone calls and a short visit; now her presence is everywhere.

The magazines arrive addressed to her. Through a series of events—settling an estate, forwarding mail, and closing a business—I get these little presents from beyond. A magazine distributor could probably explain how mailing lists and promotional giveaways play a role in bringing me these treasures of the soul, but I prefer to think some other cosmic happenstance is responsible.

The same goes for the crocus, daffodils, and other bulbs and perennials that I planted in my yard. What makes these treasures of the earth appear? Is it the angle of the sun, the temperature of the soil, or is there some other mystical reason? A biologist could explain the scientific phenomenon, but does that make it any less amazing?

The seasons play a part in the perennials' appearance as they add a backdrop to our own metamorphosis. Spring, summer, fall, and winter narrate the passage of time and give us proof of life after death. Without the seasons it is hard to tell if time moves at all. Much like riding in a car, you can't tell if it's moving forward if you can't see out the window. The seasons provide a reference point to guide our progress as they push us forward, keeping us company along the way.

But this methodical move forward can also be frightening. Like a monster in a horror movie, time never stops. It slowly creeps forward. I try to capture and hold a moment in time. I think I will remember how high the snowbanks were, how the minus forty wind chill felt on my skin, and how the snow muffled the sounds of winter. But already in spring, I will have forgotten it all. By the dog days of summer, I won't believe I will ever need a jacket again.

I am not sure it is good to have a constant reminder that we are aging. We would probably be happier if we measured our lives in seasons and changes to the earth than in birthdays and changes in ourselves. The earth has been aging for a lot longer than we have, and I think it has learned to do it more gracefully. We could all learn to offer up flowers after a long, cold winter or show off our brightest colors after a hot, humid summer.

The earth flies through the seasons while we struggle to keep up. Huge landscapes are transformed in days, and we lament a gray hair. The earth sees the bigger picture—leaves are replaced in spring and snow melts only to rain somewhere else. We take it all personally, as if the universe was created just so we could solve Sudoku puzzles and watch reality shows.

The earth knows how to take a punch. I won't go into pollution, global warming, or overpopulation. I am not worried about the earth. When we have overstayed our welcome, we will simply be shown the door.

In the meantime, I enjoy the seasons and the surprises they bring. Like magazines from my mom, I am never sure what will show up next.

- 2008 -

The Art of Shoveling Sidewalks

Forget the Fourth of July parade or summer festivals. When it comes to uniting neighbors, winter creates the backdrop. With every snowfall a fabulous thing happens. Neighbors step out of their homes and participate in the most community-oriented activity we have—shoveling our sidewalks.

Each city is comprised of mile after mile of sidewalks, not to mention driveways, walkways, and front stoops. After each snowfall, thousands of residents emerge to shovel them. It is the biggest cooperative effort most residents will ever participate in. We work to clear safe passage for our neighbors. We create a sense of community by coming together, quite literally, as we burrow our way to adjoining properties.

Maybe you help your neighbor with their sidewalk. Maybe you have the biggest snow blower on the block and run it down the whole sidewalk. Maybe you visit your parents and make a day of clearing the landscape. The important aspect is that we all come together to share the experience.

I am a purist myself and never use anything but a shovel, preferring the meditative state of moving snow with my own body. It's quiet and peaceful, straining the muscles and freeing the mind. It gives purpose to exercise and you can't beat the workout.

Using a snow blower is cheating Mother Nature. She works hard to remind us we are not in control. She can pick up our house, flood it, or bury it in snow, and all we can do is react. I feel the power of Mother Nature with each shovelful of snow I throw. Besides, a shovel won't break down, refuse to start, or run out of gas—although I might.

People in Arizona with their pleasant weather never get the opportunity to test their mettle. It is winter that brings out the best in us. We take pride in showing that a little snow won't slow us down, a bit of hard work doesn't scare us, and no matter how high the snow banks get we can still pile on more.

Winter can oftentimes be isolating as we hunker down from the cold and raw environments. It is refreshing to come outside, even if we are bundled up beyond recognition, and move snow. It also allows the whole family to get out in the snow and play. From a five-year old's perspective, making a snow fort and shoveling the sidewalk are identical activities.

On a sunny day after a snowfall, a patchwork quilt of shoveled sidewalks appears. Each snowbank tells a tale of the hard work and pride that went into it. I enjoy sitting back and admiring the results until the snow plow deposits another two feet of snow and ice to be removed.

Sidewalks are what bind us together. They not only allow us to walk safely, they represent community property we all share. It is when we forget who our neighbors are and don't care about others in the community that we begin to fear our surroundings. We need these community connections we call sidewalks. We need to greet our neighbors from them, walk along them, and in winter take time from our busy schedules to shovel them.

- 2005 -

The Breath of Life

Life is amazing. I'll go out on a limb and say living is one of the best experiences, with biting into a good wood-fired pizza a close second. I am alive. I am a participant in this sensory heaven that allows me to enjoy the texture and taste of a tart apple or feel goose bumps from the unexplained exhilaration of a forgotten song. From chemical and electrical impulses, I can string together a narrative and contemplate my existence. I not only live, I wonder.

Colors are spectacular, as if a tidy child discovered a one billion-count crayon box and worked to fill in the world, but couldn't make up her mind on what blue to use for the sky and tried them all. Growing fickler, she turned to shades of red, then upended the box, and grabbed all one billion crayons in her big beautiful hands to remind us that there's no limit to the colors of the sky.

When I sleep and my body recharges, I continue to experience wonderment in the form of a private concert, performed for me, by me, as my brain slowly chews on significant moments. These dreams make up their own rules that allow me to swim through the sky, walk through half a century, and relive high school, with or without pants.

I just took a breath. I'm told I do it often, and it was refreshing. Somehow, I took oxygen from the air with the use of muscles that I don't fully understand, in a process I don't generally notice and converted this gas to fit in my blood stream, keeping my hands and cheeks a cheery pink hue. If I breathe slowly and deeply, it calms my body in an ancient rhythmic process, my mind becomes less frantic, and I feel happier. And to think of all the events I've tried and activities I've joined, just to be as content as a good deep breath can make me.

An extra benefit to breathing, as if it needs one, is that molecules enter my nose and stimulate receptors to create an evocative response in my brain. The rewards of such a process can be summed up in one word—bacon.

Life takes a certain amount of patience to truly enjoy. We need time to catch our breath, notice a sunset, listen to our own heart beat that magical rhythm. We can worry about bills or the growing To Do list. There are always duties to perform just as cells in our body continually maintain their life-sustaining process. But who will appreciate the rosy sky as it feathers into wispy clouds?

Beauty surrounds us. Miracles happen with each breath. Holding hands connects two worlds in a sea of tactile receptors. Communication embellishes our sensory world, allowing us to compare experiences. We still have appointments to keep and chores to complete, but no one said we can't take a few moments from worrying about what to make for dinner to feel the sun on our cheek or hold someone's hand as we wait in line.

A good day isn't about the tasks we performed—how much paper we fed through the machine or the number of clients we called—it's about the amount of time we had in our busy schedules to take a deep breath and enjoy the calm or marvel at a particularly orange leaf as it danced through the air in a moment that will never come again.

Life is amazing, but comes with a limited shelf life. I have taken more than half of the roughly one billion breaths I'll ever take and I've noticed only a few handfuls.

What do you want to notice in this sensory wonderland? The dirty kitchen countertop or the amazing pattern created by the smear of peanut butter on Formica?

Breathe deep and take advantage of life. Like a slice of good wood-fired pizza, it won't last.

- 2016 -

Pick-up Hockey

It's the greatest sport around. No, not football, basketball, or baseball. I am talking about hockey. I don't care to watch it; I want to play it. A pick-up hockey game of complete strangers can materialize in seconds, including all ages and skill levels where nobody keeps score and everyone has a great time.

I played hockey the other day at my nearest park. I just showed up with my skates, hockey stick and puck. I didn't know anyone. I didn't make any plans. I just hoped for a little friendly game of hockey like I remember as a kid.

When I pulled into the parking lot, the ice was empty of players, but by the time I laced up my skates, four hockey players appeared out of nowhere. Soon we had a two-on-three game, and I was in heaven.

Players ranged in age from ten to forty with all different skill levels and sizes, both male and female. Additional players arrived along the way and were quickly recruited to a side in seamless fashion without stopping play. Soon we had a four-on-four game and the pace quickened.

Outdoor pickup hockey is a finesse game of stick handling and fancy footwork. Nobody had helmets, breezers, or shin pads. There was no checking or slap shots. It was hockey in its simplest form.

We didn't even keep score. It was not about winning or losing. It was about playing the game, having fun, working not so much as a team, but as a group of friends even though we didn't know each other's first name. It was as all sports should be—simple.

The younger players used their endurance and relentless pursuit while the high school kids used speed, skill, and size. I, being the oldest player on this particular day, used experience, size, and positioning along with some pretty fancy backward skating to put on a respectable performance. The point is we each had our strengths. The ice has a way of leveling the playing field.

Each game is different depending on where you play and who shows up. I have played with twelve people on a side or as few as two, in twenty-below temperatures or in the rain, with all older players and with all much younger, on ponds, lakes, skating rinks, and hockey rinks. Each condition challenges your skills and frees the ego.

Sometimes league kids with all the gear show up, and sometimes you get the kid who has never been on skates before. They can all play. That is what makes this sport so great. It is not about winning or losing, but trying. Without strict rules and expectations, the true nature of a friendly game of hockey can surface.

I went home after an hour and a half, just as my younger competitors were getting warmed up for another three hours of hockey. They will be out on the ice tomorrow as well. I, on the other hand, will be recuperating for at least a day or two before getting back on the ice.

Blisters and aching muscles are a small price to pay for feeling like a kid again. I also appreciate the workout, all while having the time of my life.

We need sports like pick-up hockey as a way to connect to the best inside us. So, find your puck, sharpen your skates, and tape up your stick. Enjoy the ice for a change instead of slipping and sliding and cursing its existence.

- 2005 -

Finding Truth

I like to debate. Ask almost anybody. I enjoy sharing ideas and the heightened awareness that comes from these long and sometimes awkward exchanges. But debate is disappearing, swapped for comments on social media, typed in comfortable cocoons of like-mindedness. Our lack of interest in all things difficult-to-define is growing.

When I was young, my mom encouraged me to ask questions, state an opinion, then defend it. I remember a friend of my parents asked for my opinion about a subject I don't recall. What I do remember is the feeling of purpose, reinvigorating my young self-esteem. It was then I realized that opinions matter.

For my wife, issues are straightforward. She doesn't like messy decisions. Complicated solutions are fine, just not controversial answers, and she has little time for philosophical musings. They tend to lead to wasted afternoons. Unfortunately, my wife takes the brunt of my babble, enduring my endless theories about how drive-thrus destroy civilization or why everyone should mulch their leaves.

Though answers intrigue me, it's the process that I find more telling. Data seldom comes without strings—partisan information meant to sway, inaccurate conclusions skimmed from the headlines. News has dwindled, leaving us all to fend for ourselves. We scrounge for information not tainted by prejudice or ignorance in search of wisdom.

I have a tendency to exaggerate more than anyone in the world. It's a family trait to blow issues out of proportion to make a point. Data is a delicate object, requiring a gentle touch, lest we contaminate it beyond recognition.

Ideas are wonderful things, filled with purpose and problems, but they only become real when expressed. Once ideas escape, they can be blindly followed and repeated or debated and challenged in an effort to find truth and inspiration. Debate gives words a place to grow while still pruning them when needed.

Opinions matter. We all have them, and only by combining our views do we start to piece together a bigger picture. The difficulty is sharing opinions. Conversation has become a competition where the truth is what is said the loudest and most often. Getting to the truth requires tinkering with the muddy underpinnings of opinion, clearing away judgment and other debris to see what remains

Expressing myself honestly is difficult, but the best place to start is to assume I'll be wrong and say it anyway. It's not what they taught me in school, where only the right answer was rewarded. What is truth but the culmination of thoughtful ideas presented honestly and reflected openly? I could remain quiet, afraid of being wrong, then commiserate with a few who share my same viewpoint. But I want to understand the world I live in and the people I share it with. The best way I know how is to listen and poke and prod, digging like an archeologist, trying to find meaning in the fragments of insight left behind.

I'll keep talking and writing my secrets to the world in hopes that my words find strong opponents to slay my weak conclusions and offer a bridge to new ideas.

Now let me tell you what I think about drive-thrus.

- 2014 -

The Moon's Lament

I'm so misunderstood. I circle the planet, but you seldom glance in my direction. You're too glued to your tiny screens of artificial light and busy scurrying from place to place to notice me. I have to do a full moonty to persuade a few of you distracted souls to give me a minute of your time.

It's not fair. The sun gets all the attention, worshipped, revered. What a joke. Where are all you people at midnight? In the dark like the rest of us, that's where. And who's there to keep you company through most of those lonely nights? Me, that's who. And I don't want to hear about the Aurora Borealis. It's the sun's cheap parlor trick. Wait until she goes supernova. That'll change everybody's opinion in a hurry.

Don't get me wrong: the sun and I get along fine, but we move in different circles. She needs to be the center of attention with everything revolving around her. She's distant that way, trying to entertain eight planets. You might think you're her favorite, but you're wrong. It's Mercury.

My point is, I'm always around, giving the best show I can. You won't see me flitting out past Saturn like some comet. I don't care how enchanting her rings are. I'm not two-faced. I orbit and spin at the same speed so I never lose sight of you. If that's not love, I don't know what is.

To be honest, I'm lonely. Nobody visits anymore. Not that you ever beat down the door. Twelve people in three years hardly constitutes a mad rush. But it's been nearly forty-five years. Is it something I said? Something I did? Is it that old tide thing? I can't help my sheer magnetism.

I hear you're interested in someone else. Don't think I haven't noticed all those love letters to Mars. Why is it everyone ignores what's right in front of them? They're always infatuated with the distant bad boy planet. Let me tell you from experience, long-distance relationships are brutal and Mars has an attitude.

I'm no pushover—a big, soft ball of cheese with no feelings. That Pink Floyd character got me, he understood my dark side. A few thousand years ago I was a big deal. Civilizations planned their lives around me. Poets haven't forgotten me, but that doesn't mean I've forgiven you yet.

I know how to regain your attention. I shouldn't say anything because I don't want you to freak out. Soon, I'm going to show the sun who's boss. I'll slide right in front of her, real graceful. We happen to be the same size from your vantage point even though she's over four hundred times larger than me, which only emphasizes how incredible I am.

Don't worry, I saw what happened to Pluto. I won't make trouble. I'll linger in front of the sun long enough to get your attention. I'll do a little dance, point and say, "I'm not touching you. I'm not touching you," until the sun shows some respect for my years of service to your planet.

It's called a solar eclipse, but it's me you're really staring at. You need special glasses to look at the sun, but when I'm not with her you can stare at me for as long as you like. When this is all over, let's spend some time gazing at each other. You can contemplate the wonders of the universe while I try to understand what it is you people do down there.

P.S. Visit soon.

- 2017 -

Easter Eggs

Growing up with my family, Easter was a celebration of Spring—rebirth of the perennial plant kind—dominated by eggs, and accentuated by candy.

We often visited relatives—roughly forty people in all—and ate ham while talking about things I never fully understood, spoken in a family dialect of implied meaning. A crappy new job was simply a woooonderful opportunity and scandals were traded like recipes without measurements or instructions so they could never be replicated. With a hunk of Peter Rabbit's belly or leg, I navigated the foggy landscape of cousin relationships, trying to find a conversation that bridged a four-month gap in visits and several years in age.

Easter is about resurrection—for some, of a man—but for me of life itself, watching daffodils rise from their decayed leaves six months earlier—second chances, new beginnings, infinity. Faith can come in the belief of one person's journey or the constant miracle of a yellow flower emerging from a lifeless ground. They both hint at a circular fashion to our existence and something unknowable, an Easter egg to be found.

My Easters were filled with eggs. My mom would hard-boil twenty dozen eggs and we'd gather around our oil-cloth-covered table. Implements of decoration were scattered about—crayons, markers, wax, pencils, and whatever else could be found in the big box of debris from Easters past. My mom used food coloring and experimental dyes to get the most vivid colors. No one could leave the table before completing at least a dozen eggs.

Easter egg coloring was a competition to see who could come up with the funniest egg pun or best color combination or most unique technique incorporating fingerprints. Participants changed every year—neighbors, cousins, unsuspecting friends who thought they could color one egg before an evening of bar hopping only to leave two hours later, fingers ten different shades of dye that wouldn't fade for days.

The next day we would eat blue deviled eggs, the dye having seeped through the shells, but first we had to find them. As the youngest, I raced around the house for the sheer sense of discovery. My older siblings were too cool to look, but they seemed to know where all the eggs were before me. They still had to find their Easter baskets. My parents met the challenge of know-it-all adolescents, hiding my brother's basket in the garbage can, under the bag, and my sister's hanging from the shower head. I vividly remember at least one egg we didn't find until sometime in July, hidden in the drapery.

I don't color many eggs these days. I figure I've dyed my share for a lifetime. But I haven't outgrown candy. When I was younger, candy was all powerful, or at least I thought. I later discovered my candy appreciation was downright amateur compared to my in-laws, who still speak of candy in hushed words of reverence, reminiscing about sugar scene eggs and their favorite Baby Binks chocolate bunnies. They lament the loss of candy from their youth—Nice Mice, Black Jacks, Turkish Taffy—and talk fondly of trips to Bowlby's Candy store, walking home with their white bag of penny candy.

They decorate their walls with old chocolate boxes from See's and shun new-fangled flavors like sour jelly beans and watermelon Peeps. If it isn't Brach's, then they aren't real jelly beans. When Brach's was sold, a collective shiver ran down their entire family's spine. They all have their own secret stash of jelly beans or circus peanuts or candy corn, depending on the season—the hard stuff. They debate chocolate shops as if they are comparing colleges, each with their own set of criteria.

I look forward to our annual trip to Hughes' Chocolates in Oshkosh. We like to go when it's busy, the line forming in the driveway as we're packed like sardines in a basement too small to be useful yet holds fifteen of us while six pots of chocolate stir continuously. My wife and I try to control ourselves, working in tandem, but we always buy more than we'd agreed upon five minutes earlier in the car.

Jelly beans and oysters from Hughes' are as welcome as daffodils and coneflower, and all are equally predictable, yet mysteriously amazing in their own resurrections.

- 2015 -

Background Pieces

At times we will find what we need,

or reach a balance, or come closer to

understanding ourselves, but these triumphs

come not from where we stand,

but how we got there.

"Graduation Speech Never Given"

Time Capsule of Youth

Deep in my closet I have a time capsule—a cardboard box filled with treasures of my youth or debris from the journey, depending on the sentiment. From all of my childhood possessions and memorabilia, somehow this one box is all that remains. This isn't scrapbooking, more the product of a lack of planning and a need to jettison weight from all the moves I've made. I seldom open it. The box is more a comfort. I like knowing it's there, physical evidence of my existence.

If I could do it all over again and hand-pick each item from a pristine supply, the box would be filled quite differently, but that would be missing the point. It's the difference between a candid photo and a posed picture—one is real life, the other is not. Most people have a similar box in their own closet with an equally confusing array of items that somehow describes them as nothing else can.

Inside are the standard high school yearbooks filled with pictures of students I vaguely remember three decades later. Across some pages are written comments about how glad they are to have met me and advice to "have fun." Though the connection to pictures, names, and memories is vague, the emotions are strong. I'm left with a general feeling of regret mixed with the loss of something valuable that I can't quite remember, as if I once had a treasure map but have now misplaced it.

This is why I keep the box, to revive a whiff of my younger self. It's also a reminder of old friendships and fuzzy dreams as I search for some understanding of the years gone by. Though I don't want to remember everything—hence only one box—I do want to continue picking at the scab of my adolescence, feeling just a hint of pain while removing the crusty outer layer.

This box also contains my high school and college diplomas along with a mold of my teeth before I got braces. I have several papers from school: my favorite are my life story at age eight and my philosophy of life written my freshman year in college. Apparently, I didn't like green peppers and onions and thought women were confusing. It's like going back in time and talking to my younger selves. Unfortunately, I can't shake any of these younger versions to make them understand. They can only guide me from their limited but unique perspective.

I have various art supplies from when I went through my creative phase. I couldn't bear to get rid of them and give up on the dream of being an artist. Just having them in my box preserves the illusion that any day I could turn out works of art regardless of how dried out the paints are. They are a placeholder of the little piece of artist I carry within me.

One of the most boggling items is a small box of buttons, the kind with sayings you pin on. It started from a collection I got from my grandmother—a few buttons pinned on a long piece of felt—now a pile of rusting metal. Why I hang on to them I don't know, except they connect me to the past, linking generations, as if the buttons themselves were clues to my ancestor's whereabouts.

A transaction book from my first savings account is hidden among the items. The account was opened in 1974 with $50. I closed the account in 1982, the year I graduated from high school with $607.40. I made $108.77 in interest. Other savings and checking accounts were shuffled off into one of my financial boxes, but this account was different. It was my first visit into the grownup world and started my love of saving.

A few pieces of refrigerator art remain with bent corners, yellowed paper and a few phone numbers scribbled in the white spaces. Refrigerator art was never meant to last, so even these beaten up samples have value. They represent the ever-changing self, given prominent position at the center of the fridge only to be replaced or moved as the next version came along.

I have a few more odd and ends, a couple of healing stones from a mystic stage, a small sewing kit from a hotel I never visited, and a little green cloth grasshopper with a top hat given to me when I stayed in the hospital for a week at the age of eleven. Like pieces of a meteor that survived reentry, these items are a random collection of what survived my blistering arc into adulthood.

It's time to close the box now. These items were never meant to be examined for too long. They're like a defibrillator, only meant to jump-start the heart, not pump for it. Back into the closet they go to act as my talisman, protecting me from wandering too far from myself.

- 2012 -

Bullying

Bullying is all the rage lately. It's so pervasive we don't recognize the antagonistic behavior. Whether we repeatedly gossip about a colleague or taunt a beleaguered classmate, these seemingly small events can have immense impact. Bullying is everywhere—school, work, home, politics, TV, even in our religions with claims that my God can beat up your god. In life's unfair system where power reigns over kindness, it's tempting to dismiss bullying as an inevitability, designed to toughen us up for the hard knocks of life.

Every one of us has been affected by bullying. For me, I was lucky. In school nobody bullied me. I had an older brother and was therefore pre-bullied, making me immune to most threats any student could deliver. But I do remember a time in high school when I picked on another student. He was the student considered safe to pick on—everyone did. I can't remember what I said or why.

What I do remember is a friend of mine didn't approve of my behavior. He didn't let it slide, or worse, encourage my bullying with a smile. He certainly didn't join in. Instead, he challenged me. He pointed out that I was being an ass. He let me know it wasn't OK. It wasn't safe to pick on the kid that everyone else picked on. My behavior was not appropriate and he made sure I knew it.

That was more than thirty-five years ago. How many events do you remember from your high school years? How many experiences resonate three and half decades later?

This one does. I don't remember my friend's exact words, but I remember the feeling. I remember the sense of shame. It was as if he pulled me out of some other reality. One minute I was funny, powerful, in control. With a few words, my friend showed me I was pathetic, abusive, out of line. I was a bully.

His words made me look inside myself. I remember wondering why I had even done it. I had never harassed this person before, nor was I one to torment any student. But I did. Other students were picking on him as well, making it seem more acceptable. Luckily for me, my friend pulled me out of my self-induced crowd-enhanced stupidity. He saved me from drowning in my own ugliness.

Sometimes only a friend can make us see our own weaknesses. His words didn't come across as a lecture or boring advice or input I could ignore. He was on the inside, on my side, leaving no barriers for his words to overcome. His comments stung because I could not dismiss them. His intervention succeeded because he happened to be one of the very people I wanted to impress with my rude remarks.

We all have it—the ability to bully. We are equally susceptible to being bullied. We base our perception of the world so heavily on other's opinions. We yearn for approval like a puppy learning new tricks. We think we can gain approval by showing our superiority over another. We only show how afraid and lonely we really are.

The only solution to the fear and isolation we all experience, is compassion, not superiority. We need to help each other see our own follies, pick each other up, and help those trodden by our unkind words and deeds.

It's the least we can do for a friend.

- 2016 -

Little Things

Tucked between birthdays and retirements, weddings and funerals, are the moments we commonly refer to as the little things, those day-to-day experiences that make up a lifetime. Our achievements are wondrous, but few and far between. Even our disasters, while often painfully drawn out and relived, are equally as sparse. It's moments like quietly drinking coffee, emailing a coworker, or driving the kids to soccer practice that make up a day. These small events often go unnoticed and unappreciated, but lately they've been catching my attention like bright red maple leaves in autumn.

Fall does that to me, reminding me that small things have incredible power. Leaves fill out a tree and give it shape yet are only paper thin. These same leaves provide shade in the summer while converting the sun's energy into food. Only in the fall do we take notice when they turn bright yellow, orange and red as if teaching us that many little things can be spectacular.

I seldom appreciate the amazing colors of my days. Moments like reading a book or searching for my phone are quickly raked away. But in the fall, as the sunlight filters through the multicolored leaves creating that special glow, I see my days differently. This particular day will never happen again. Like a single leaf that drifts down from its summer perch in a slow seductive dance, I can either ignore it or tango with this impetuous partner.

A happy person isn't the one with the most money or power, but the one who is the most comfortable sitting alone. When we can't bolster ourselves with achievements or drag ourselves down with failures, we're left with our true selves. Comparing and competing may push us to achieve more, but it doesn't make us happier. Jealousy reveals areas within us that are not at peace. Envy isn't a tool that hones our abilities, but a weapon that weakens our self-image.

Life isn't only about how we handle success and failure, but how we handle the absence of the two. If we keep busy enough, maybe we can pretend we're not worried. If we crank up the drama, perhaps we can postpone contemplation. If we over-stimulate ourselves with technology, hopefully we won't have to feel anything at all. We're not good at harnessing the power of silence or wringing out the joy of a car that starts, a friend who smiles, or a leaf that turns an orange never seen before.

Boredom is the worst thing to inflict on a kid. When growing up, I'd rather annoy my big brother until he made me cry than be bored. It's only when I've gotten older and my brain cells are more saturated that boredom is a welcomed friend, a quiet time to sift through the day's events. I remember in my teens running place-to-place looking for the excitement that eluded me as if it was wild game, never realizing excitement wasn't a thing to find, but an experience to create.

I can be happy about a hot sunny day or feel miserable depending on whether I'm at the end of a long winter or a hot summer. I stood watching runners come into the finish line of a half marathon recently and noticed a participant upset with his time. Thirty minutes later a woman finished and was ecstatic. More runners came in hours later, many equally euphoric. It's not about feeling disappointment or excitement over any particular event, but the realization that life provides the experiences and we provide the emotions.

I used to hum while I ate as a kid, reveling in the pure enjoyment of the simple act of chewing. Now I eat with purpose or with no thought at all. I plan what to make for dinner. I calculate the time between meals to determine what I should eat next. I think about nutrition, leafy greens, and bad fats like baseball statistics. I no longer listen to the music of eating a crunchy meal. It's hard to enjoy the little things with all this planning and goal setting going on, and it's even more difficult when we work so hard to make them more complicated.

People create bucket lists to catalog big achievements and thrilling adventures they want to complete before they die. Seldom do we make lists to study our wife's eyes or be conscious of how acorns feel when crunched underfoot or listen to a noisy room full of people for that magical hum. We reach for the novel, the hard-to-find, ignoring the stockpile of experiences available every day. Distance and frequency can be misleading, blinding us to the exquisite so close at hand.

Fall is our yearly reminder that incredible things are all around us. We only need to notice. Leaves, like us, are only here for a short time. It's not how long we cling to the trees or even how graceful we fall to the ground that matters. It's how we choose to experience the journey.

- 2012 -

The Warmth of Downtowns

We take our downtowns for granted. We forget they're an endangered species. Downtowns aren't just a series of buildings: they're an energy source, a lifestyle that slowly forms a patina from decades of use. Each downtown is unique and personable with a special magic that holds a community together.

My wife and I went searching for a community several years ago. We weren't hunting for jobs. We were looking for a place we could wrap ourselves in—an extension of ourselves. We found that peace and personality, all within walking distance to a lively downtown.

It didn't take us long to realize the power of the approachable downtown that is big enough to give off energy, but small enough to allow residents to warm themselves in its glow. Downtowns may seem ordinary to those who only drive through them. I find them to be true gems repeatedly rising to the surface of an ever-changing landscape.

They hold us together, become our fortress. They entertain us, feed us, distract us, and make us feel welcome, yet downtowns constantly struggle to keep our attention. We cheat on them for a two-dollar savings. The formulaic and overloaded discount and big box stores lure us away with the seductive promise of lower prices, and we head for the door without a backwards glance.

We come back to downtown for the parades and festivals and fall in love all over again with the lights, music and community. We wonder why we continually ignore our downtowns as we slow down momentarily for our drive-thru coffee on our way to the freeway.

We all need a destination, somewhere to go, a place to belong. Sometimes shopping isn't about buying stuff. It's about spending time together and conversing about the weather or the health of a neighbor. We need to talk to that person at the cash register and look them in the eye instead of staring blankly at our receipt while talking on the cell phone.

We continue to keep our downtowns at arms' length. We move farther away, not closer. We slowly weaken our downtowns with shopping centers and strip malls. We strive for more space as we gobble up precious farmland and environmentally sensitive areas.

We think distance doesn't matter—five blocks are the same as five miles, driving is the same as walking or biking. It's not. Driving downtown is a little like texting a hug to your kids. It's a nice gesture, but it loses the personal connection. Living within walking distance of downtown creates an intimate relationship. Once you get in the car, who knows where you'll end up.

We don't want our downtowns to go away; we're just a little too busy to use them right now. We're busy moving out to the suburbs with three-car garages. We think they'll always be there when we come to our senses, but we might be surprised by what we find. Either everyone is having fun downtown without us, or we've strayed one time too many and our downtowns have up and left us.

- 2008 -

The Mystery of Grace

I hoped for a fast checkout in the grocery store and when I saw no one in line, I wondered if I had just spent one of my wishes. In the spiritual world of hopes and wishes, prayers and karma, I don't know how they are doled out or by whom. I'm not presumptuous to assume I know what force or entity is involved or if any exist, but for the purpose of this conversation, let's call her Grace.

I doubt Grace has an unlimited supply of petty wish tokens she hands out like raindrops to whoever asks. I have always thought of wishes as both limited and fickle. I say fickle in part because I don't understand the process. Sometimes I want the signal light to stay green until I pass, but it doesn't. Other times I ask Grace to hold back the rain for a few hours and she does. It's not as if my voice carries more weight. I imagine Grace sends out surreptitious surveys on the need for rain and uses some convoluted scoring system.

Even though I don't know how it all works, it doesn't stop me from making requests. Like learning a new app on my phone, I push every button in sight. The tally for this year alone is nine green lights, five bike rides with the wind at my back, three occasions when time somehow extended itself, allowing me to make meetings on time, and one avocado that appeared in my fridge when a moment earlier I saw none. I try to ration my wishes. I'd hate to run out and never find my keys again.

I'm not even talking about the bigger wishes. I say a prayer for my brother and know my parents cashed in whatever tokens they had to keep him safe when they left this earth. I wonder if wishes and prayers for other people are unlimited. I don't want to know the answer. It might influence how I act and I'd rather my actions be more spontaneous than anticipated. It's when we expect results or are certain none exist that all hope is lost.

The unknown makes prayers and wishes more powerful. Like days of my life, if I knew how many I had, I'd live them differently, squandering years if I knew I had many or fretting about having too few. I'm uncertain if Grace is listening and I'm sure she has better things to do, but I keep speaking to her. Like kids calling only to ask for money—at least they call. Maybe the reason I do it, make these petty pleas, is to remind me of life's mysterious marvels hidden behind this curtain of small outcomes.

These curious coincidences make good practice for the real thing, like biopsies and skidding cars. But when disaster wraps its arms around me, prayers turn to desperate pleas to make the pain stop. I seek to bargain, not find wonder. Dread of what I know overshadows hope from what is unknowable. I'm tempted to cling to dogma, but it threatens to smother the wonder of finding a parking spot right in front. I feel more comfortable believing in the unknown than picking from one of the pre-packaged options. It's more familiar to me and more hopeful.

Have faith in what brings you hope. Embrace possibilities and never stop believing signal lights stay green a little longer just for you.

- 2017 -

Shopping with My Wife

Shopping with my wife is an adventure, if not a bit complicated, filled with points and precautions. We each have our own style of perusing and strengths in procurement that aren't always compatible, but are usually entertaining. We help each other navigate the retail maze of promotions and pumped-in perfumes to keep our sanity.

Our experience begins in the expansive parking lot where we each have our favorite place to park. I like open space, but she prefers the first available spot, wedging the car between two trucks. I make that noise men make to indicate disapproval while hoping it sounds like an innocuous sigh. She's not fooled. My shopping points start with negative numbers.

I wait for my wife to do whatever she does for five minutes before she gets out of the car, then I bolt when she opens her door, conveniently forgetting the defective mattress pad in the trunk. I have issues with returns, as if I have the flaw, not the product. My wife braves stares and finger pointing while approaching the service desk, unintimidated by the judgment I'm sure is taking place in a monitor-filled security room.

In the store, I like to travel light, but my wife—who wrote the list—insists on a cart, which would be fine, except she leaves it in the middle of the aisle or double parked, not acknowledging cart etiquette. So I push it with the left-pulling wheel, trying to see past the eighty-four pack of toilet paper—the smallest size the store sells—hoping I don't knock over another display.

My wife believes in using all five senses while shopping, opening every package, breaking through the engineered labyrinth of plastic and cardboard. She needs to touch the fabric, smell the shampoo, hear the vacuum cleaner, while I quietly look for an excuse to be somewhere else. I could shop by myself, but then I'd miss the entertainment of watching her unfurl a queen-size memory foam mattress topper in the center aisle for inspection.

Finding my wife in a store is impossible. She's short enough to hide behind any display and has an uncanny ability to be at the opposite end of the store than our agreed-upon meeting place. I usually wait until I hear a vacuum cleaner or see lights blinking in the lamp area to find her. We compare selections, talking the other out of their ill-advised, marketing-hyped choices. My wife has a tendency to return unwanted items to inappropriate shelves, placing the rejected shirt next to the DVDs. I focus on the TVs and try not to notice.

Candy is my wife's Achilles' heel, and I have the Herculean task of keeping her away from it, stiff-arming her as we near the Easter candy. It's a delicate balance—take the Robin's Eggs from her hand and be called heartless or ignore the two-pound bag of jelly beans she later slips into the cart. I have no issue with jelly beans except I'm the one who must endure the week of agony as she comes down from a sugar high and chemical-induced psychedelic trip, docking me fifty points for letting her buy them in the first place.

I can't take my wife grocery shopping. It's not just the candy; she's unaware of what food looks like uncooked and makes a scene at the raw chicken parts. I hold up romaine and red leaf lettuce, but she's already bored. She doesn't understand the sense of urgency at the deli either, thinking we have more than two seconds to decide between a half and quarter pound of ham.

I'm no shopping angel either. I have a tendency to linger in the meat section and ride the carts. I'm shopping-list-impaired, always forgetting something, and I have a phobia of coupons, returning home with crumpled clippings in my pocket. I wander, looking at the DVDs when I'm supposed to be getting paper towels, and I can't distinguish the whitening-mint-freshening-gel-massaging toothpaste from the other thirty-five varieties.

Shopping can be challenging, but my wife and I team up to resist shampoos that rejuvenate, select the softest sheets, and analyze the growing packages containing shrinking products. It's a chance to spend quality time together and can even be romantic as she stares longingly at me. I just need to be standing in front of the chocolate bunnies.

- 2014 -

Graduation Speech Never Given

"To be or not to be," that is the question asked by William Shakespeare in *Hamlet*. "What to be or what not to be" is the question for high school seniors with every spring.

Graduation is the crossroads between child and adult. Suddenly your life is not so much in others' hands as your own. While the options seem limitless, so is the pressure to do something with your life. The only question is—what?

There is no shortage of answers, and the question is not limited to high school seniors. We all wonder what to do with our lives. At forty-three I still have not figured out what I want to be when I grow up. The problem is not the lack of answers, but the question. It is not what you want to be that counts; it's how you want to live your life that makes the difference.

We assume some perfect job exists for each of us, and once obtained everything else falls into place. Not so. The only final destination is death itself and I, for one, am in no hurry to arrive. At times we will find what we need, or reach a balance, or come closer to understanding ourselves, but these triumphs come not from where we stand, but how we got there.

We never figure it all out. Time only helps whittle away the clutter. Each year brings a keener sense of what is important. As we accumulate knowledge, gain success, and enjoy accomplishments, we fill holes in our lives, but some areas are harder to reach. We're forced to look within ourselves instead of out there among the gurus, experts, teachers, and parents.

If we're lucky, we find a harmony in our lives and an appreciation of the process. We stop racing against each other and enjoy the meandering journey to destinations unknown.

There will be plenty of advice given at graduation: work hard, get a good education, follow your dreams, see the world, get a job. While these are all solid recommendations, they are not very helpful in addressing the subtle issues of the unknown or the overpowering reality of change.

You will make your own mistakes. You will learn things I will never know. You will see things that no one should. You will have dreams that others do not understand. You will live a life that is unique and completely your own.

It isn't as if your lives have just started. You have had eighteen exciting years of experience, enough to get a sense of who you are and an idea of the complexities you face. There are so many new choices available and the cost of miscalculating is greatly accentuated by your distance to the finish line. The fear is that any misdirection in the early stages can lead you completely off course later in life. Don't give in to these fears.

Life is the most crooked of paths. While it is true that the shortest distance between two points is a straight line, life is not measured by distance. It is more important to get where you need to be while enjoying how you got there, or at least appreciating it. You are going to have to backtrack, take the road less traveled, and sometimes blaze your own trail. Even if you know where you are going, your destination isn't always where or what you thought it would be.

Decisions do not limit your opportunities. If you major in psychology you can still be an architect. If you go to tech school to be a welder, you can still be an artist. No experience is wasted. In contrast, choosing nothing does not leave all your options open. It is not our decisions that limit us, it is time and energy. Stand still long enough and life will decide for you.

Be bold. You are not the rat in a maze trying to find the cheese. Because the truth is, there is no cheese, only a maze of choices and the search to find ourselves.

- 2008 -

Colorful Pieces

-defined by their color and grouped together-

The one who felt our sweaty forehead,

held our trembling hand,

and soothed our growing anxiety,

can bleed and cry, and still find time

to teach us humility through

her honest stumble towards death's door.

"Tough Lessons and Long Goodbyes"

Hash Browns First

Every moment in life is a learning opportunity, if we only stop and look for it. Every job we've ever had taught us lessons that last a lifetime. On my first job I learned one of the most valuable lessons of all—Hash Browns First.

Today Fortune 500 companies spend years studying popular concepts like Lean and Six Sigma to reduce waste and eliminate defects. An entire industry has been created to teach these techniques, but nothing compares to working as a short order cook to bring these concepts to life. Slaving over tens of thousands of food orders brings a Zen-like understanding to these complex ideas.

I got my first crash course in production methodology as a sixteen-year-old cook at Perkins Family Restaurant. Wearing my hairnet and smelling of burnt grease, I was ready to take on the world. In reality I was just trying to get through another grueling shift short-handed and sleep-deprived.

I found myself alone in the kitchen early Saturday morning and the place was packed. I had fifteen food orders in front of me with more coming in every few minutes. I had developed a good rhythm as I worked on three or four orders at a time, but I was just keeping my head above water.

It's important to understand work capacity. Work on too many orders and food burns or gets soggy. Work on too few and the waitstaff will eat you alive.

Food has its own order and rhythm too. Eggs cook fast but require the most prep work, so they control the flow. Pancakes are quick, but timing on the flip is critical. Bacon takes time and makes a mess, and hash browns cook the longest.

I had two big grills going. One was completely filled with twenty-four pancakes, recently flipped. The other grill contained four hash browns, three omelets, a dozen eggs, and sixteen strips of bacon. The four-slice toaster was down and twelve plates were garnished, waiting to be filled. I put together the first two orders and started on the third. I was on fire.

Then disaster hit. I forgot to put down the hash browns for the third order. Production came to a halt. I couldn't send out the order without the hash browns. I salvaged what I could and started over. By the time I finally completed the order, I was buried and never caught up.

I learned a lesson no book or management class could teach. I witnessed the relationship of events. I looked beyond the eggs and bacon and understood the intimate dance. It doesn't matter how fast you move if you don't follow the right steps. Speed must be tempered with an understanding of the process. I could rename all the events and throw in some impressive sounding theories, but I would still be left with one simple lesson—Hash Browns First.

The lesson went beyond management theory and became an analogy for life itself. Life has its own order. If you try to rush things without understanding the process or think you can go straight to the eggs of life and put the hash browns down later, you will find you have created something unappetizing.

Seventeen years later I was plant manager of a large printing company with two hundred employees. Instead of food orders, we produced store signage for some of the biggest retailers in the country. The process remained the same. The projects were just bigger—as were the consequences. I often remembered that Saturday morning at Perkins and the lessons I learned. Working hard did not guarantee success. Understanding process and flow was crucial.

Hash Browns First became my mantra. Every project I ever worked on, whether a million-dollar signage order or painting the house, I analyzed through the eyes of that sixteen-year-old, to the point where I can sometimes still smell the burnt grease. Even going for a walk now is a strategic endeavor to pick the most advantageous route and maximize sunlight. I can't watch a neighbor mow her lawn without thinking of more efficient patterns.

Those first jobs are important, providing the foundation for our later successes. They may seem trivial, but between the hairnets and aprons, I learned the most important lesson of all—Hash Browns First.

- 2008 -

Misjudged Winter

Winter is the black sheep in Mother Nature's family, the troublesome offspring causing problems for motorists and a royal pain in the butt for all in his presence. It isn't Winter's fault; he tries to behave, partly a victim of birth order. I hold no grudges. I understand his purpose. Someone must keep the cockroaches and termites at bay. I just wish he'd take it easy on the rest of us.

It's his attitude of course, 23.5 degrees to be exact, slouching away from the sun, unwilling to participate. As the youngest, he's always had a difficult time fitting in, made to stand in the corner, an unfortunate time-out for us. I can relate to Winter, a born introvert, gathering energy from solitude, yet he is still resentful when so many avoid him and head south.

Winter is lonely and incapable of warmth. I sometimes feel the same, shivering inside, isolated. If I were a season, forced to pick last after all the good leaves were gone, would I be any different? Would I not rebel if I was left with only hand-me-downs and weary parents, obligated to make amends for my siblings? Summer has to take some blame, breaking curfew, and Fall waltzes by, receiving all the compliments. I don't blame Winter for being resentful.

I try to enjoy Winter, but every year I become more annoyed at his cavalier attitude, dropping his clothes wherever he likes as if I were his servant. I resent shoveling the sidewalks and driveway, cleaning up his mess. When we go out together running or skiing, he gives me the cold shoulder, making me feel uninvited. Even the sun doesn't want to be around him. He doesn't understand how his negative attitude affects others. I often make excuses, staying inside just to avoid awkward moments, cursing his name as he persuades my car to misbehave.

Winter has his good points. He covers decrepit gardens and frosts trees until they sparkle. He washes away insects and kicks out the riff-raff. I should feel honored to be his select friend, but I know it's only because I'm one of a few who can stand him. He does have a sense of humor, playing tricks with water and ice. He just doesn't know when to leave, not taking my subtle hints. How many times do I have to say, "Is it Spring yet?"

I try to be patient like the moon, searching for hope, witness to the simple beauty of an owl hovering in time as shy shadows dance across fresh snow. Winter can illuminate, strip away hiding places, lay down a fresh blanket to reveal covert operations. I'm amazed at the bunny highway that crosses my snow-covered patio, clearly showing I'm not nearly as alone as I thought.

Winter never cared much for appearances. He's too practical, no bright colors or fancy foliage, just white. He strips me of my color, dries my skin, and rubs my head until my hair sticks up in the most unappealing angle, simply as a reminder to be less vain. He still holds a grudge, believing I was mocking him in my adolescence by not wearing my hat and gloves and now follows me around, breathing down my neck, making my skin sting, a reminder of my youthful foolishness.

I want to learn from Winter, how to sit still and gain strength. Instead I expend energy over-thinking life, missing the simple message of steam rising off the river. I look for the meaning of my existence by what I have accomplished, never fully appreciating what I experience. Falling snow isn't an inconvenience, something to shovel, but messages encoded in water droplets from Peru, love letters in crystalline form.

Winter is misunderstood, seen as a bully when he's the one who has been mistreated: cursed, hated, abandoned. We've done it all and much more. But we attempt to make it up to him every four years with the Winter Olympics, seventeen days of winter frolicking. We slip and slide on the ice and snow and make it into a ballet, an art form. I'm not as graceful in the parking lot, but give myself an 8.2 on a spectacular wipeout and find a little of my own winter gold.

Winter might be lonely and misjudged, but he knows how to dish it out. The more we embrace Winter, the kinder he becomes. I just wish he wouldn't hug me so tightly.

- 2015 -

Tough Lessons and Long Goodbyes

Caring for a dying mother is not for the faint of heart. Death seldom sneaks in, silently scooping up our loved one before tiptoeing out of the room. He kicks down the door, breaks windows, and makes a mess. Death holds friends and family hostage while he prepares the dying for their journey. We punch and scratch and claw at death, taking out bites in a tug of war we can't possibly win, yet we never fight harder. Ever. When he eventually leaves, taking what we so desperately cling to, he sucks all the air from the room, our weary bodies gasping at the inevitable.

We can feel Mom's absence in a missed kiss or an errand we no longer have to run. We think about what we want to tell her about our day, only to remember she's not there to answer the phone.

Dying is that between time, when Mom transitions from the all-knowing parent to the somewhat forgetful adolescent to a distracted toddler. The regression, while never quite linear and varying in length, is meant to prepare us for her eventual departure. It's like saying goodbye to faraway friends. We need a good hour to reminisce for the third time, to hug each other, ensure they have snacks for the drive. And still we linger on the back stoop, then in the driveway, and finally watch until their car is out of sight.

As with most long goodbyes, when the door finally closes, we are left exhausted, wondering about our departed guest's journey, if they made it safely, if they're home yet. No one likes long goodbyes, but we tolerate them: anything to keep our loved one close at hand, if even for a little longer. Dying can be the most awkward of long goodbyes, drawing out the agony of the final separation, sometimes for years, leaving those behind regretful they didn't say or do one more thing while guiltily wishing their guest would leave already. It's impossible to give enough, to say enough, wishing we could have tucked away one more treasure for Mom to carry home.

Parents—mothers in particular—do what they have always done, teach. They remind us to say thank you and please, they explain how to behave in public, and in the end, they show us how to die. It's not pretty or graceful, and dignity can be difficult to maintain. But they teach by example, going first if they can help it to show us the way, like testing the playground slide for us when, as kids, it seemed far too tall. They demonstrate what it means to be stubborn and tenacious, clinging to life and us so we know what true challenge looks like.

They drop their guard and let us peer into their souls, revealing a vulnerability we didn't think they were allowed to have. The one who felt our sweaty forehead, held our trembling hand, and soothed our growing anxiety, can bleed and cry, and still find time to teach us humility through her honest stumble towards death's door. How we wish it could be simpler, easier. But our moms would tell us nothing is harder than the protective coating a mother forms around her children and to break it, for a child to see the mother clearly, you will need a very big hammer. Death is a sledgehammer.

Some believe our mothers are in a particular place and that we will one day reunite with them. I like to think they are everywhere, part of the cardinal, daisy, the air we breathe. Perhaps I can't wait so long to see them again, thinking moms shouldn't be limited to where they can go. After the battles they have fought, the sacrifices they have made, they should be allowed to roam and play and discover, peeking at us from endless vantage points.

No matter where moms go, their impression on us is great, leaving marks. To all moms who have gone before us, and especially Val and Julie, whose departures have and will continue to teach us the understanding of loss, of love, and the art of the long goodbye, we say thank you for the tough lessons and the wild ride.

- 2015 -

Armchair Traveler

I just got back from my spring break trip to Mexico. I had a great time: I relaxed, hung out with friends, read some books, and saw incredible scenery. The travel was problem-free and I saved a boatload of money. I even drank the water. What is my secret to a relaxing and cheap vacation? It's simple. I never leave Neenah.

Call me an armchair traveler. Much like armchair quarterbacks who don't need to be flattened by a three hundred fifty-pound lineman to feel a part of the game, I don't have to travel great distances, wait in long lines, pay large sums of cash, or get treated like a criminal at the airport to feel the excitement of getting away.

With a good imagination and a philosophical look on life, I can climb Mount Everest and still sleep in my own bed at night. It's all about attitude. A vacation isn't so much about the destination, but the escape from everyday life.

A record snowfall and a fabulous white sand beach have many things in common. They're both vast, sun-drenched landscapes where your feet sink into the terrain in a satisfying way. Though there are no dolphins to watch, lake sturgeon have their own appeal. I don't need to worry about bugs, hard-to-reach sunscreen areas, or aggressive salesmen on my beach.

Eating out makes a great vacation getaway in itself. To add a little tropical flair to the sub-zero trip, try wearing shorts, sunglasses and a colorful shirt. Order drinks made with coconut and pineapple. Dessert is a must. Just the right amount of chocolate can transport me to the rain forest. If I'm not careful I might develop an uncontrollable urge to buy a destination t-shirt.

Once home, turn up the heat, put on a swimsuit, and crank Jimmy Buffet while pulling out the blender. Invite friends over. Flying two thousand miles doesn't make us any freer, just more jet lagged. Escape the ordinary by traveling the much shorter distance from purposeful to playful. This moment would be the same anywhere in the world. It's not defined by scenery or weather, but by the company we keep and the layers we shed.

Relax in the luxury of time. Even grocery shopping can be an exotic excursion when time and attitude are adjusted. Forget the list and instead watch everyone else rush around. Feel the bubble of peace that surrounds you. Buy vacation food like shrimp, pomegranates, and funny little jars of peppers. It's still far less expensive than eating at a resort. Test all the product samples, listen to conversations, and contemplate the larger questions in life like who makes it rain on the vegetables in the produce display.

Drive slowly and enjoy the scenery. We travel thousands of miles to slow down and look at other people's scenery. Instead, take time to see what is around us every day. At a stop light, refrain from making phone calls or multitasking. Enjoy each moment, don't fill it up. We're normally in such a hurry. Sometimes all we need to feel on vacation is to slow down and be more deliberate.

Nothing says vacation more than doing nothing at all. A vacation is the only time we're allowed such an indulgence. We run ourselves ragged all year in hopes of one quiet week, but with missed flights and a jammed itinerary, we often need a vacation from our vacation. This vacation do less and enjoy more. Go nowhere, plan nothing, nap often.

For those who simply can't sit still, vacationing is also a time to explore new things. When friends visit, we usually take them to places we've never been to ourselves. We think there's nothing left to discover here, but we've barely scratched the surface. Now is the time to act like a clueless tourist. Ask dumb questions, wander into the wrong places, get lost, and make discoveries.

My mom always said that no matter where you go you always take yourself with you. Yet we somehow think if we change where we are, we'll change who we are. We believe new scenery will make us calmer and happier, as if our problems develop outside ourselves like the weather.

We can travel great distances in hopes of finding this new us or we can look inside ourselves. With the willingness of a traveler, the hope of an explorer, and the spontaneity of a tourist we can all reach that internal destination where the weather is perfect and spring break is only a piece of chocolate away.

- 2009 -

The Rule of Rules

I live my life by a certain set of rules. These rules aren't designed to bring about world peace or raise my existence to a higher plane. They've simply developed over the years from an overactive need for control and a misguided belief in my own self-importance.

Hidden in the obscurity and convolution of these rules emerges a philosophy that everything is connected and underneath the mundane lies an intricate path of poorly reasoned associations. It's not that I always have to follow these rules, but I feel better if I do. They exist solely in my head and in theory I could eliminate them tomorrow, but it's not that simple. They have become a part of me. I could no sooner rid myself of rules than use a drive-thru.

Just going places can be tricky. My rule is to always walk or bike wherever I go, unless it's below thirty-five degrees or icy or too far or I just don't feel like it. If I do drive, parking is an issue. There's a complicated set of rules about parking too close to other cars or the entrance or waiting for a parking space or crossing the store's pedestrian sanctuary, all causing delays that make me feel guilty for driving in the first place.

Grocery stores are equally challenging. Cart etiquette is crucial. I can never block the aisle even if the store puts up a hundred displays, making it like a maze to navigate. Canned goods must never exceed the amount of produce in my cart. A three-to-one ratio is preferred. Never buy frozen entrees, peanut butter containing sugar, or anything from the bakery other than bread. I can't even walk down the soda isle for fear of high fructose corn syrup poisoning.

When I'm sick, I can never say out loud that I'm sick. My body would hear me and act accordingly. It's best to pretend nothing's wrong—nothing to see here, move along germs. One advantage to being sick is the rare opportunity to watch TV while it's still daylight. A Packers game is the only other exception, but only if it's below forty degrees or inclement weather, otherwise I can only listen on the radio while working outside. I can also only sleep in bed during the day when I'm sick. I can nap on the couch whenever possible because a couch is daytime furniture and immune from time.

At a restaurant I can never order the same food as anyone else at the table because eating out is a communal quest in which each participant must explore new territory. Always order to a restaurant's strengths—never a salad at a tavern or a hamburger at a fish fry. Never order anything I can make at home in less than fifteen minutes. Fast food isn't food.

When cooking at home, never run out of food when guests visit, even if it means making three times too much. I always include a vegetable with dinner; canned corn and beans don't count. Never use margarine, shortening, tomato paste, or baking powder. They're either poison or cheating. Never throw food away without a cooling off period. No matter how moldy or smelly it is, examine it, put it back, then throw it out a week later when it's beyond recognition.

I never rake leaves to the curb. They must be mulched, even if the piles are three feet high. Always shovel snow instead of using a snow blower. The only exception is if it's a really heavy snow and no one is looking. Then I borrow my

neighbor's while they're gone and pretend it never happened. Never spend more time caring for the lawn than the
gardens. Flowers can be pampered, but the lawn is meant
to be walked all over.

The list of unofficial rules goes on and on. I am constantly creating more as new situations arise. Most of my
rules exist at a subconscious level so I'm not even aware of
them. Those are the hardest to break, but I have a rule
against breaking rules.

In a world already full of too many rules, it's odd that I
would devise more, but sometimes it's nice to have some
things you can call your own, even if they are more rules.

- 2015 -

Happy Hour with the Canadians

I spent five days on the Florida panhandle coast in an RV park with my sister and her husband. RVs make for cramped living conditions, but the sense of community was even tighter. Something unique happens when people from all over the US and Canada are condensed down to a well-packed RV park. With seemingly nothing in common but the love for the road and a fondness for meeting other people, you get Happy Hour with the Canadians.

At 5:00 sharp, twenty-plus people met for happy hour. Everyone was from a different state or province, but it felt more like a family reunion than an impromptu get-together of strangers. That's because they were anything but strangers. Many had been coming to this same RV park for years and staying for months.

Being new to RV life, we were welcomed as if we just had married into the family, learning where everyone was from instead of who they were related to in this would-be family. The conversation was refreshing with no agenda or sense of time. No one bragged about their career or their kids. Business vernacular like synergy, fruition, and critical mass were absent. If there was any bragging, it was about the number of miles traveled or states visited.

It was pure conversation, undiluted by commercialism. There were plenty of bad jokes, lots of cheap beer, and a few "ehs" from the Canadians, but it wasn't so much about the words spoken as it was about the time shared. We got to know people not just by what they said, but how they listened and the way they hugged their dogs.

Time played a big factor. Most of the people were not on vacation for a week, but for months, years, or a lifetime. Taking out the garbage became a three-hour process of wandering from one conversation about the best place to get shrimp to another about the dark side of Bingo, only to get on the same merry-go-round of conversations coming back to the RV. No one looked at their watch or tapped their foot. These casual chats were not filler in a too-busy life, but the main event.

The day wasn't about what you could get done, but what you were doing. Once the brain stops calculating the next six tasks that must be completed, it can focus on the person in front of you, and if you have nothing to sell, you are left with conversation.

The Canadians even had a quaint way of recording their favorite TV programs. They had one of their friends watch the program, then tell them all about it. If nothing else, they at least avoided the commercials.

If you really want someone to talk, don't use waterboarding: put them in an RV park. A person can only spend so long in a small RV after being submerged in winter for months. Once outside with all the time in the world and the first rays of summer sun, you almost can't keep your mouth shut. Add in several other people from even colder climates and you have yourself a gab fest.

It takes a certain sophistication to enjoy an RV with the cute little fridge and miniature sink. It's like playing house in your own pretend home in a make-believe neighborhood or hatching adventures in a secret clubhouse, making the RV park more like a playground than campground. I wasn't taught the secret RV handshake, but I joined in the fun just the same—campfires around the propane torch, storytelling, water fights, and climbing the lighthouse.

Even rolling out an awning became a spectacle for community advice and ritual. Everyone had an opinion and was not afraid to give it on wind speed, torque, and angles. With the technical nature of RVs, the topics are endless—from tanks and slide-outs to hydraulics and hook-ups—everyone was willing to help whether you needed it or not.

RV living breeds the best supervisors. With all that time to think, it's only natural to solve everyone else's problems. The RV management was re-landscaping a section of the park with eighty palm trees and hundreds of shrubs. Little did she know twenty additional supervisors would be overseeing the project. I quickly got caught up in the excitement, calculating the best order to plant and how to compensate for the weather.

It's easy to get carried away at an RV park with its care-free timeless atmosphere and magical sense of community. You quickly lose yourself in another world where grownups act like kids, conversation is an art, and everyone enjoys life one happy hour at a time.

- 2010 -

Loving Libraries

Libraries are magical destinations and cornerstones of a community. They promote learning and stir the imagination. They offer a place to sit and relax, read, surf, borrow, meet, learn, and listen. For young or old, libraries are the last frontier of discovery, where great works of art we call literature can not only be touched but taken home.

I am lucky enough to live within walking distance of my local library. It is my home away from home, my playground, my community center. I read these strange scrolls called newspapers and find recipes in magazines I've never heard of. Mostly, I watch and listen to other people, taking the temperature of my community. I could read the newspaper online at home, but then I might miss a couple discussing Johnny Carson or the erratic path a toddler takes as he follows his father. I would miss the buzz of the city around me.

The library is the one place with the largest cross section of the city's inhabitants. Every age, every occupation comes through the library doors, all looking for knowledge, but always finding much more. We find a connection to the world that we couldn't get through the internet. With all its connective power, the internet isolates us in our solitary searches. The library mixes us into the fold of humanity.

When my wife and I travel, sooner or later we end up at the local library. While others race around to see the tourist sites, we casually lounge in comfy library chairs and take in the town. All the answers can be found among the shelves, artwork, and the people. Each library is different, with its own story to tell and a personality that reflects the community that it serves.

During our honeymoon we spent many hours in, of all places, the library. On Mackinac Island in the pouring rain, we found solace in the small library on the Lake Huron shoreline. The storm carried on outside while we relaxed among the books, mismatched chairs and roaring fireplace in a romantic moment of silence and safety. It was refreshing to take a moment away from the tourists and fudge to slow down and unwind.

There are not many public buildings that encourage you to linger, but the library is designed for it. The library's main purpose is to provide for the community. They supply not only comfy chairs, but reading material to boot. There is no time limit on your stay, no one is trying to sell you anything, and you are not required to perform any tasks.

It is one of those rare opportunities to explore like a kid. There is no end to the surprises hiding on each shelf. Read about the making of Gilligan's Island, look at the graduating seniors in the 1946 yearbook, or choose a CD solely by the picture on the case. The library is like a big treasure hunt with clues, mystery, and rewards you can actually hold in your hands.

You will never find anyone as helpful as a librarian. Ask them anything. If they don't know the answer, they know where to find it. It is like having Alex Trebeck, Oprah, and your favorite science teacher all rolled into one. If you are looking for a book by an author with a female sounding name that starts with a P something, they can find it. They might not be able to give personal advice, but they can find a book that can do that.

Libraries don't simply contain books and movies; they contain all that we have put into them. They hold the past, present, and future of a community. They give us somewhere to go to search for our dreams and find a little of ourselves among the shelves. In this over-commercialized world, it's nice to know there still remains a place where all are welcome, questions are encouraged, and items are meant to be borrowed, not sold.

- 2005 -

Hidden Pieces

-the piece we hide to be the last one put in the puzzle-

It's not always good to know where we're going.

No roadmap can guide us

to places we don't know exist.

They can only be found in our hearts.

"Get Lost"

Falling

I don't remember being afraid of heights. When I was eleven, I regularly challenged my next-door neighbor, Jimmy, to see who could jump from the highest tree branch into the snow, sometimes twenty-five feet below. I climbed with abandonment and flung myself from precarious perches, flying for a few brief seconds before a foot of snow and bad judgement caught up with me. As my knees collided with my chest, momentarily knocking the wind out of me, I didn't connect the fall to my inability to breathe. Instead, I climbed a taller tree.

A person's mind doesn't fully develop until twenty years of age or later. That might explain my gap in reasoning then, but not my fear of heights now, in my fifties. It started on the Zippin Pippin rollercoaster a few years ago—that slow, methodical, clacking ascent, foreshadowing gravity's revenge. I stared at my hands, clutching the bar instead of admiring the incredible view of Green Bay. As I reached the peak and plummeted down, I might have let out a scream—terror or exhilaration—who would know? Certainly not my wife with her hands in the air. On my third ride, I wondered what happened to that kid who wanted to fly.

My problem worsened when painting the outside of my two-story house over the summer. I reached a distinct step on the ladder beyond which my body would not go—far below the highest branch I'd ever climbed. I stopped, one foot halfway to the next ladder rung, a bucket of paint and brush in one hand, the edge of the ladder vise-gripped in the other.

If I wanted to paint my entire house, not just the lower half, I needed to overcome my fear. And fast. Paint was drying. I went up and down the ladder several times, painted where I could and slowly tricked myself into believing I was only a few feet off the ground. My legs shook and I painted outside the lines, but I did it. Not just one coat, but two.

I'm not left with a feeling of accomplishment as much as a reminder of how I've changed, how life has left its impression on me, how my favorite color as a kid was once bright orange and now it's smoky blue. I'm reminded that I still like to fly, take gigantic leaps, but now I do it with words and ideas. I sometimes find myself stuck between two places, afraid to move forward as if one wrong step could send me tumbling to the hard, paint-splotched asphalt below.

It's not so much the fall I mind. It's the landing—the cruel reality of my limitations. My body has minimal protection, but it's this vulnerability that gives me strength and forces me to climb or find another way around, to appreciate my limits so I might understand myself. I learned I have no desire to paint a two-story house ever again.

Whether on a ladder or in front of a computer, I can't fool myself. I can pretend I am not getting older, but my body knows better and reminds me often. Circumstances change with time to alter perspectives and distort distances. Holding tight to the nearest stationary object offers an illusion of control, but I go nowhere. To move forward, I must keep on climbing and leap into the unknown, hoping I fall with grace and eventually catch my breath.

Ready? I'll race you to the next branch.

- 2018 -

Memory That's Got Soul

We were never meant to remember everything. Forgetting isn't only a defense mechanism that saves us from our most painful memories, it reduces the clutter of a million experiences a day. Though memories aren't perfect, they're surprisingly helpful in capturing and prioritizing the true essence of a moment. It's this process that defines who we are and provides a unique souvenir of our visit here.

We don't store data like a computer, in a purely mechanical way. While computers can be more precise and better with numbers, they lack a certain human touch. We're flesh and blood and rely on a more personal process of electro-chemical impulses that are laced with emotions. Data isn't stored alphabetically or chronologically, it's stored emotionally. A first kiss won't be cataloged under F or K, but under scary or thrilling or both.

Dramatic moments are highlighted in emotional red ink and always kept on the desktop for quick retrieval. Even if they are surreptitiously buried, these bulging files are sure to be disturbed from time to time, spilling the contents across the floor. Routine moments like oral hygiene are scribbled in light pencil that quickly fades.

Sometimes the emotion encoding isn't perfect. When meeting new people, the flood of data and emotions can short-circuit the system so a person's name is lost before it can even be forgotten. Nothing is remembered with complete accuracy, but processed through our own interpretive lens, like watching a conversation in a foreign language and guessing what is being said.

Photos and home movies are unnatural. They're physical reminders that never quite match up to our biological storage system. In our ever-changing, touchy-feely world of emotions, pictures are a stagnant and cold intruder. Photos bring with them a clarity our memories aren't meant to convey, while at the same time missing all the emotional content.

An old photo might elicit an emotional response, but it's tainted by time and distance. Younger faces and forgotten fashions distract me from the true taste of the ice cream cone in a twenty-year-old picture of friends at Baskin Robbins. New emotional connections are forged, like feeling embarrassed by your overly tight jeans in the photo when at the time you felt invincible. The true essence of the memory is traded for a few shiny baubles of detail.

We want to remember everything so we can relive the memory. It can't be done. We bang our heads against the wall trying to remember high school graduation. We can piece together people and places, but we lament the things we can't recall. It doesn't matter. That experience has already been lived and filed away. It's like trying to take eggs out of a sugar cookie once it's baked.

Each experience builds on the others, blending and changing our contents. We're never the same. We carry with us the emotional elements of graduation day, adding flavor and texture to our lives, but, like the cookie, the experience no longer remains intact. We live a moment only once, and are left with the emotional aftertaste.

Memories are stored in this emotional cookie batter for two reasons. The first is survival—providing quick access to the most important memories. When the car is sliding on ice, we don't have time to search through a thousand records of uneventful driving days. We want immediate access to all files labeled driving-out-of-control-on-ice. Luckily the panic folder is always on top with blinking red lights.

The second reason is portability. Memories are stored as emotions so they can be taken with us when our bodies have kicked us out. Emotions hold much more data than a photo or computer ever could and take up such little storage space as to be somewhere between a whisper and thought. If a picture is worth a thousand words, then an emotion makes those words redundant.

Our experiences define who we are. Our brains might block certain memories and have physical limits that impede retrieval, but the experiences still glow inside us. Like going on vacation and thinking you forgot to pack your swimsuit, only to find it in your suitcase when you got home, our experiences are always with us, even if we can't find them.

Quantity and quality don't matter. Whether we lived one day or one hundred years, created great works of art or caused pain, we take it all with us. While our individual actions may be judged by those still clinging to the details and physical demands of this world, our accumulation of life experiences moves forward as a single entity that is valued for only one thing, its uniqueness.

While a computer might be more efficient for storing facts and figures, it can't handle the emotional complexities required to represent who we are. Our system of storage isn't perfect, but like us, it's got soul.

- 2013 -

First Decision

We're defined by our decisions. Even if each choice is influenced by a complex array of variables we never fully understand, we become owners of those decisions all the same. Often, we're unaware of decisions we make, responding automatically out of habit. Occasionally one stands out. I remember my first. I was seven years old.

My older brother and his friends were leaving to play hockey on the pond behind the neighbor's house and I wanted to join them. My mom didn't want me to go. I was too young, the ice too thin, the air too crisp, the world too hard. My mother, wise in the ways of children, or perhaps the residue of a guilt-infused Catholic upbringing, didn't forbid me from playing hockey. She let me choose.

She explained her rationale, making it very clear she didn't want me to go. She also made it equally clear the decision was mine. My mom was big on equality—no one had all the answers, and every idea could be challenged no matter the source.

With barely a glance backward, I put my stick and skates on my shoulder like the big kids and headed down our driveway. Halfway down I felt the weight of skates on my shoulder along with a much heavier responsibility of my first decision—hockey and fun or Mom and approval.

My mom was the center of my universe, and like the sun, she lit up my world, almost blinding me with her motherly radiance. She didn't pamper me and knew exactly how far to push. On this occasion she didn't watch me walk down the driveway with a disapproving look. Instead she quickly walked into the house.

With her no longer there to defy, I was left with a decision that wasn't simply a reaction to her, but based on my own set of values. Even at a young age I recognized guilt, but at the same time I sensed the glory that could be mine on the ice. My mother wouldn't love me any less if I played hockey, which made it even harder to disappoint her. The less she pushed, the more I became responsible for my actions.

My brother walked faster and I wanted to match his stride. If he had picked on me or encouraged my choice, it might've changed the balance between guilt and glory. I was caught between two immoveable objects that were both, ironically, moving quickly away from me. The chance to impress my older brother and become his equal was fading as quickly as my mother's words.

My steps down the driveway became less confident until I finally came to a complete stop. I couldn't move forward or back, caught in the pull of these two masses. The pressure was crushing. I was inexperienced with implications. Logic was only a rough concept and useless in this situation.

My brother looked back, wondering what the holdup was. After seeing no blood or severed limbs, only the goofy look on my face, he continued his march to the pond. From his viewpoint I could only be a liability. I couldn't tie my laces tight enough by myself, I'd certainly get cold faster, and I couldn't even stick handle, using my hockey stick more to hold myself up.

My mom wanted what was best for me even though she realized that it would likely not be best for her. She understood my limitations and my brother's lack of empathy. She would probably feel my discomfort in the cold January wind more than I would. She knew all the possible dangers and played out every scenario regardless of the odds.

In a few more steps I would've escaped my orbit around mom and been gliding in the expanding space of freedom and hockey. But as it turned out, I didn't have the energy to break free of her gravitational pull. She gave me choice and respect, and with it, tightened the bonds that held us together. After a short pause I ran back home to show my mom that I could see the bigger picture as well—that a choice was larger than one person.

If my mom were still alive, she wouldn't be moved by this story. She would be mortified, seeing her obvious manipulation. For me, it was my first real decision—the first time I could openly defy authority even if I couldn't tie my own skates.

What I remember most isn't the outcome—I forget my mom's reaction. My biggest impression was the trust and faith she placed in me regardless of outcome. It's a feeling I carry with me, affecting all my decisions and giving me the confidence to state an opinion and question an assumption. It turns out decisions can sometimes be harder than ice.

- 2012 -

The Give and Take of Giving

Some say it's better to give than receive. I say, you need them both. They each have their challenges. One cannot exist without the other. The joy of giving a gift at Christmas, or any time, is the reaction of the person receiving that gift. They give with their enthusiasm and joy, while the person who gave the gift receives that heart-warming feedback.

Giving has its own intrinsic rewards. It's not always easy—giving of our time, ourselves, our money—but nothing else brings such tranquility. Nothing strengthens our self-esteem like helping others. Giving connects us to one another, allowing us to be seen. Giving strengthens a community not only in a physical sense—buildings, computers, and paper clips—but spiritually through bonds of caring and hope for all. It's this shared sense of commitment that reveals our true selves and strips away barriers.

Giving can take many forms—as simple as a smile, as cheap as our time, as easy as writing a check. It's the act of reaching out in any form that counts. When people dream about winning the lottery, one of their first thoughts is who to give money to. They want to help. They want to make a difference. Here's a secret: you don't have to win the lottery to make an impact. Giving isn't about an amount of money. It's about the connection, stretching, giving a bit of yourself in the process.

Receiving is the other half of the equation and an equally challenging half that I struggle to embrace.

Receiving involves absorption, making room for the gift. Even a smile requires recognizing the need to connect, then accepting the gift. It shouldn't be difficult, accepting what others give freely. It only requires the acceptance that we are not complete on our own, that we are part of a much larger community. It sounds easy, but it's not.

Think of your family, your closest friends. What creates these tight bonds? Vulnerability—revealing our weaknesses. We all need something, but we generally hide our limitations. To make one's self so vulnerable as to ask for help is a gift and the other half of the equation that makes connections possible, allows friendships to grow, and deepens relationships.

Being a receiver, asking for help, is to open ourselves completely. We risk rejection, one of the toughest forms of isolation. But if we want to connect, if we want to grow, we need to leave ourselves defenseless at times. We need to risk. We need to give up some part of our fortress to make room for someone else's kindness. It's through this exchange that both giver and receiver become whole and the equation balances.

Give what you can, understanding that nobody gives without receiving as well. Don't brush off a thank you. Let it in. Be as gracious in receiving as you are in giving. The two go hand in hand. Embrace your needs and in doing so, let others in. Open yourself to allow gifts to come in like needed nutrients.

We all need something. Luckily for us we can find what we need in each other.

- 2017 -

Packing and Pep Talks

We are all dying. We know this. But it's a slow process that generally takes decades. We don't notice the changes at first—not sleeping through the night, extra time to recuperate. Other times the dying process accelerates. When I learned I had stage IV colon cancer, I could almost feel my cells changing. If death is a location, then dying is how we get there. The destination does not bother me as much as the journey.

Traveling in general can be a nightmare of security checks, long flights, and confusing directions. But when your destination is death, the journey is bound to be even more problematic. I'm not sure of the exact route from living to dead, but I'm sure it's not designed for comfort.

I guess it's pain I fear—the loss of control, unpleasant procedures, my body failing me—the dying process condensed from thirty years down to one. Instead of walking down thirty flights of stairs, I'm forced to leap. I want it to be fast. I don't want to linger, caught between places. I'm just trying to ease the jolt of the landing.

As I pack, I realize all the items I can't take with me—friends, family, the memory of biking through the Netherlands with my wife. I, alone, must take this journey and leave so much behind, far earlier than I would've wished. As the youngest of four kids, I remember going to bed early while my siblings stayed up, most likely to eat ice cream and play cool games. As my death approaches, I have that same feeling, as if I must retire while everyone else goes for endless bike rides on sunny afternoons.

Dying is our time to prepare for our journey, but I don't even know where death is. I envision dying more like the first time I had to jump in the lake. I was afraid of leaving stable footing on the dock and landing in a new paradigm of fluid motion. I tried to give myself a little pep talk. As I contemplated possibilities, my brother pushed me in—problem solved. Death occurs somewhere between chanting "I can do this" over and over and a bigger hand doing what my body couldn't.

I hope I can find a graceful death without the need of a push or the lonely self-encouragement. I have no need to drag this out. I don't like traveling in life, so I'm certainly not looking forward to an extended journey to death. I've had my time to prepare, even if I didn't know exactly what I was planning for. I've been a connoisseur of life and a contemplator of death. I've known how lucky I've been and how short life is.

I often wonder if a part of me saw this diagnosis coming seventeen years ago, when the first cell in my body altered and began to grow out of control. I knew then to quit my job, sell our house, and search for a more deliberate life. My parents' deaths, both when they were far too young, might have been a catalyst, but I think my body understood and sent instructions, guiding me to slow down and appreciate the smell of spring or the fall of an autumn leaf.

I have lived with purpose, in a loving relationship. Friends and family have been wonderful. I have enjoyed my life. I never planned to live forever, and I've seen enough people die to believe the stories—we are all dying. Life is but a glimpse and our journey is not about our destination, but how gracefully we transition from one place to the next.

Don't push. I've been giving myself a pep talk for years.

- 2020 -

Get Lost

I have no sense of direction. I get lost a few blocks from my house. I don't have a GPS in my car or a smartphone to rely on. As it turns out, I like being lost. I find adventure in not knowing where I'm going and enjoy the sense of discovery along the way. It may not be the most practical approach to travel, but it's the best way to find myself.

I always think there's a great restaurant hidden on some back road near my home that only certain people know about and has the best smoked brisket and pepper pot soup served in a comfortable, open atmosphere. It's such a unique place nobody talks about it for fear that it will become an unimaginative chain restaurant if they do. The only way to find it is to take every exciting side road and follow a path of rambling discovery where intuition is the guide. I want to find that restaurant.

I can't get lost when I'm with my wife. She always knows where she is, using some kind of internal guidance system similar to how monarch butterflies find their way to Mexico. Every time I think I should turn left, she points right, knowing the words left and right have no meaning to me without a hand gesture. It's a challenge trying to get her lost, driving down the most obscure roads until suddenly she is no longer a passenger, but an explorer like me driving through the African bush in search of the rarest flower never seen by human eyes.

Unfortunately, my wife can also read maps and carries a large supply of them. But even maps are an adventure these days, unfolding the outdated hieroglyphs and trying to decipher the colored lines without some computerized voice ruining the whole experience. I've been told where to go enough without needing to hear it from a computer. If Lewis and Clark had used a computer, they'd still be circling Kansas City.

My wife plans, but she plans with an explorer's heart. She uses the sun and stars to guide her and is always prepared. A rare trip to the mall, all six miles of it, requires provisions in terms of water, snacks, sunglasses, lip balm, notes, more snacks, and additional layers of clothing, just in case we get stranded for a week along the way. I complain while portaging the third load to the car, but I'm the first one to reach with trembling hands for the cashews after shopping. Who knew buying clothes was more exhausting than running a marathon and more dehydrating than crossing the Sahara Desert. I spill water down my shirt, gulping the rejuvenating liquid.

When I'm lost, I could be driving anywhere—among the pastures of Vermont or the French countryside—pretending to look for cheese while on a secret mission of national importance. Every car in my rearview mirror is of course following me, so I need to make quick turns down unfamiliar roads whenever possible to elude them. Just when I'm about to save the world from a cheese monopoly, I turn down a familiar street and the illusion is broken. The operatives fade away and my trip to the grocery store commences.

I'd rather not get into a car at all, preferring to walk or bike to most destinations. It's harder to get lost on foot, but I can manage it. Even if I know where I'm going, it's always an adventure. From stopping to chat with neighbors to taking a shortcut no car could make, walking and biking are more intimate, offering several layers of opportunity for excitement. It's not so much about getting lost as it is finding new vistas and vantage points from which to view the world.

It's not always good to know where we're going. No roadmap can guide us to places we don't know exist. They can only be found in our hearts. Other times we stumble upon great new treasures and simply fail to see them. I'll keep getting lost in hopes of finding myself—and possibly that fabulous restaurant.

Now, where was I going again?

- 2013 -

Paying My Respects to Fall

Fall is impetuous—rifling through her closet, looking for the perfect winter outfit with only one thing in mind—change. She tosses aside her colorful garb for something less showy and warmer while the harsh wind blows, scattering leaves and carrying change imbued in the breeze. I breathe deeply, taking in decay and smoke from a chimney a half mile away. Trees prepare for winter, pulling in their welcome mats, discarding their baubles and decorations as I try to grasp my relationship with time. Are we friends or simply acquaintances?

It's a revolution. I watch the chaos in the streets, foliage decimated, plants ripped from their homes. The agonizing cry of defeat howls in the crisp air until I think I'm the only one alive, the last living creature in a dying landscape. I wonder what is to come of me. When will be my time? Or am I the universal witness, here to give meaning by the simple act of experiencing each leaf's fall from grace?

I feel the change now on a cellular level—aging—each experience making room in my body, displacing energetic cells, filling me with wisdom, if only I can use it. I'm not sure what the wind is whispering or what jokes the grass tells. The trees and I share some common building blocks—carbon from the same dinosaur—communicating through particles too small to see. When I close my eyes and concentrate, I remember the language.

It has no gender or tense, only purpose, and a presence that connects me to a secret world, a hidden existence. Beneath the cooling earth and encrusted surface lies a map, a plan. I can only decipher a few common words; the rest I must infer. I smile at its beauty without understanding the full meaning, like laughing at a joke when I've only heard the punch line. My spirit is lifted and among the dying leaves, I experience joy.

I attend to the transformation, mulch leaves, prepare beds, pay my respects, tending to things I don't fully understand. I feel compelled to do my best. I follow the property line, rake my share until the wind reminds me that it doesn't stay within the lines, that life is messy, chaotic, one big party to clean up after. And nature knows how to throw a party. I'm invited, of course, but I feel like an outsider. I never know what to say when asked my opinion about asexual reproduction. I generally blush and change the subject.

The sun observes me from her many hiding places, taking furtive peeks at angles I'm unaccustomed to, surprising me with her flexibility. She points out areas of interest—a lingering flower, a fluffy seed head, a leaf threatening to jump. When the sun shines on me, I wonder what she is trying to say, and I must rely on the remaining flowers and decapitated stems for a translation. They gasp out a response, but how can I believe a blade of grass that I've mutilated for the past four months?

I've learned to pay attention more to what plants do than what they say. Grass in particular is a ravenous rumor monger. Thankfully the dandelions are gone, no longer spreading lies about me. I'm told of change, of transformation, but the purple coneflowers, brown and crispy, can tell by the look on my face that I don't understand decay. I don't have the vocabulary to appreciate the subtle nuance of rot. They rock in the air, adamant, as they try to explain the underlying connections—about the shared material that time continually runs her fingers through, lovingly shuffling the elements.

I stop listening and instead wait for spring and proof of these outlandish stories. I have upset nature, not taking her advice. "We had this same conversation last spring, remember?" she tells me. Yes, I recall the discussion and the endless meetings all summer long. But fall gets my attention with her sense of urgency, appealing to my irrational fear of endings. I'm too excited in spring to think, take summer for granted, and sleep through most of winter. Now I cling to familiarity, afraid of what the wind might blow my way. I am ready to negotiate.

It's only in fall that I realize I'm the purple coneflower, the rose bush, the maple tree, waving in the breeze trying to get attention. I'm not the witness or the judge or the time keeper. I'm part of the contents that time runs her hand through to be redistributed, waiting for the day when I am everywhere.

- 2013 -

Acknowledgements

I'd like to thank my wife, Ellen, who made every one of these stories better, first by proofreading each one multiple times, then by challenging me to be less obtuse, and finally by sharing her life with me, providing fabulous colorful pieces to my puzzle. To my family—Julie, Al, Michelle, Therese, and Mark—for the unique experiences only shared by families, particularly in those early years before we knew better and learned how to hide the last piece. To my friends and neighbors who shared a piece of their selves with me and in turn enriched my life and my stories. To the many readers over the years who encouraged me with their own pieces of wisdom. To the *Post-Crescent* newspaper for giving me a stage on which to perform. To Carol Hollar-Zwick who once again made my book look as good as it sounds. Each of these stories contains a bit of me. I share them in hopes that they find a home and continue to connect us all.

About the Author

Christopher Kunz is a writer, small-city philosopher, and had been a community columnist for the *Post-Crescent* newspaper for over ten years. He moved from Minneapolis to find his community in Neenah, Wisconsin, where he lives with his wonderful wife, neglected lawns, and impossible gardens. He is the author of the novel, *Doing Time*.